"Will and Lisa are provocateurs of imagination, writing from a desert where folks are thirsty for more than the American dream. This is a much-needed invitation for justice to flow through the suburbs like mighty waters and bring to life all the parched souls trapped in the ghettos of poverty and wealth."

Shane Claiborne, activist, author, *The Irresistible Revolution: Living as an Ordinary Radical*

"Will and Lisa have joined talents to offer a compelling argument for living justly in an unjust world, and for loving our neighbors in a hands-on, life-changing way. If story is what speaks to your soul, Lisa weaves throughout these pages one fictional family's journey toward a more Christ-centered, less me-centered lifestyle. If an impassioned presentation of twenty-first-century, worldview thinking is your style, Will has that covered with a historical, biblical, and practical approach to social justice. As Will writes, 'It's hard to convince the world that Jesus cares when we don't.' With heart and head firmly grounded in the gospel, Will and Lisa show us how and why caring for our neighbors truly matters."

Liz Curtis Higgs, author, *Bad Girls of the Bible*

"Will and Lisa Samson's new book, *Justice in the Burbs*, is a moving book. I read the book and wept with recognition of the deep need for justice in this world of violence, inequality, and suffering. I read the book and wept with recognition of my own complicity in the typical reluctance of comfortable Christians to act with justice. But most of all, I wept with joy, knowing how many people will be moved to join the work for justice God has already begun in the world. The combination of Lisa's compelling narrative and Will's deep analysis, along with punchy reflections by a host of top Christian thinkers, is a perfect setup for raising the *j* word in your church. Justice in the burbs? Yes, but don't stop there! This book calls for God's justice everywhere!"

Christian Scharen, director, Faith as a Way of Life Project, Yale Center for Faith and Culture, Yale Divinity School; author, *One Step Closer: Why U2 Matters to Those Seeking God*

"Whatever happened to the vital social and moral energies of the Christian faith? They are alive and throbbing in this book that shows how the gospel can walk the missing sidewalks and unfriendly cul-de-sacs of the suburbs."

Leonard Sweet, Drew Theological School, George Fox University, www.wikiletics.com

JUSTICE IN THE
BURBS

Emergent Village resources for communities of faith

An Emergent Manifesto of Hope
edited by Doug Pagitt and Tony Jones

Organic Community
Joseph R. Myers

Signs of Emergence
Kester Brewin

Justice in the Burbs
Will and Lisa Samson

Intuitive Leadership
Tim Keel (October 2007)

Losing My Religion
Samir Selmanovic (Summer 2008)

www.emersionbooks.com

JUSTICE IN THE BURBS

BEING THE HANDS OF JESUS WHEREVER YOU LIVE

WILL & LISA SAMSON

BakerBooks

Grand Rapids, Michigan

Published by Baker Books
a division of Baker Publishing Group
P.O. Box 6287, Grand Rapids, MI 49516-6287
www.bakerbooks.com

Printed in the United States of America

Library of Congress Cataloging-in-Publication Data
Samson, Will, 1964–
    Justice in the burbs : being the hands of Jesus wherever you live /
Will and Lisa Samson.
        p.   cm.
    Includes bibliographical references.
    ISBN 10: 0-8010-6809-6 (pbk.)
    ISBN 978-0-8010-6809-6 (pbk.)
    1. Christianity and justice. 2. Social justice—Religious aspects—
Christianity. 3. Suburbanites—United States—Religious life. 4. Evan-
gelistic work. I. Samson, Lisa, 1964– II. Title.
    BR115.J8S36 2007
    261.8—dc22   2007007418

In keeping with biblical principles of creation stewardship, Baker Publishing Group advocates the responsible use of our natural resources. As a member of the Green Press Initiative, our company uses recycled paper when possible. The text paper of this book is comprised of 30% postconsumer waste.

green press INITIATIVE

ēmersion is a partnership between Baker Books and Emergent Village, a growing, generative friendship among missional Christians seeking to love our world in the Spirit of Jesus Christ. The ēmersion line is intended for professional and lay leaders like you who are meeting the challenges of a changing culture with vision and hope for the future. These books will encourage you and your community to live into God's kingdom here and now.

From the beginning of the Christian faith, the agenda of God has been intended for all the world. And people of faith were called to proclaim the justice of God "in Jerusalem, in all Judea and Samaria, and to the ends of the earth" (Acts 1:8). There is no limit to places of justice, and there is no place outside the scope of where justice should be lived.

In *Justice in the Burbs*, Will and Lisa Samson lead a crucial conversation about how we can all lead lives of justice in the obvious and not-so-apparent places. For those who feel that justice is an issue for only the urban center, this important book creates a vision and plan for living justly from the city to the suburbs and to the ends of the earth.

Emergent Village resources for communities of faith

This book is dedicated to
Bill and Arlene Samson,
who taught us to how to radically follow
Jesus wherever he might lead.

Contents

Introduction

Our Story—from Will's Perspective

We failed.

We wanted to say that from the start because questions of success have such huge significance in our culture. It's the dedicated athlete, soldier, or businessman who becomes the motivational speaker. They will give you some formula with three or five or seven steps and tell you they know this success formula works because it worked for them. They may even make some promise as to what they believe their method will do for you.

We cannot do that. We failed to live a life of justice in the suburbs, and this book is, at least in part, our *mea culpa*— our confession of insufficiency.

Ironically, that insufficiency may give us a unique vantage point as storytellers. The contemporary tale of justice seems to be one with few chapters and even fewer happy endings. Perhaps this is why the title alone, *Justice in the Burbs*, gets such a great instant reaction when we mention it to people. We all have this sense that we are to be participating in writing God's story of love in the world, and yet it can be very difficult to know how, particularly in the suburbs.

Regarding our citizenship in the burbs, we are both insiders and outsiders. We are insiders in the sense that until very recently, we lived all of our lives in that setting. We lived, worked, raised children, and labored in churches, all in the context of the suburbs. We are products of the American suburban experience.

But we have increasingly sensed there is something missing from that experience. This perception of the missing element, and the quest that flowed from it, brought us out of the suburbs and into the city of Lexington, Kentucky, where we now work with various communities of need. So in that sense, we are outsiders. We personally needed to move out of the burbs for a time.

We have begun to see the problem of suburban justice in new ways. If you have seen the movie *The Matrix*, you know there can be objectivity from stepping out of a system and looking in. It is our hope and prayer you will benefit from our vantage point of having lived most of our lives within the suburban matrix and now having the rare opportunity to look back in.

It isn't our intention to tell you our whole story. But it is our intention to speak from our experience. It will be woven throughout the book in the hope that it will be useful as an example.

Somehow, as we became adults, we did not see the story of justice as a part of the story of God. How did that happen? And why?

A chronology of events would not serve to answer the "why" question completely. We could talk about our churches, our parents, our schools, our friends, our communities. All these life elements were formative in who we are and how we think, but they would provide only a part of the answer. Providing those historical details may even go a long way in answering the "how" question. But it is insufficient to answer the "why" question.

The question of why we came into adulthood with an incomplete understanding of God's story is more nuanced and involves much deeper questions than we will ask in this book. Part of the answer involves what we were taught about the Bible. We both grew up in churches that emphasized Scripture memory. Yet neither of us can remember ever memorizing a verse about God's concern for the poor. By the time we left our homes for college, we estimate that we heard more than four thousand sermons between us, and we had attended church or chapel more than any other activity except class. Yet neither of us can remember hearing sermons about God's concern for those in need during these formative years.

Does God care for the poor and for those left out? Can his care be discovered through reading Scripture? And, if the answer to those questions is yes, why were those truths not part of our spiritual formation? This is one of the questions we will be exploring in the pages to come. We suspect our experience had something to do with the view of God that the people in our churches held.

Before you make assumptions about our families, let us assure you that these were good homes. We attended churches where our parents were active. Our families were engaged in their communities. Our mothers were at home when we got off the bus from school. We had good, religious homes where we were taught the Bible and some notion of our role as Christians in the world.

Yet somehow we grew up with little or no instruction about God's heartbeat of justice. We received no teaching about those within the church who have fought for and written about justice—Dr. Martin Luther King Jr., William Stringfellow, and St. Francis of Assisi, just to name a few. Beyond the Bible, we had little exposure to church history and the many stories of those who have spoken of and worked for justice as they lived out God's story.

Lisa and I are coming to learn that many writers and workers within the church saw issues of justice as deeply related to their understanding of God. In fact, as we will explore in greater detail later, the detachment of one from the other is a relatively recent phenomenon.

We tend to believe that the way people act privately, publicly, and communally says a lot about who they believe God to be and what they believe God cares about. If someone harms their body with drugs, on some level they have a view of God that is, at the least, insufficient to prevent them from acting in that manner. If someone votes for a particular political candidate, on some level they believe that the candidate will act in ways that are consistent with what they perceive God to care about. And if someone is part of a community that does not speak about or act on issues of justice, they are affirming a belief that God is not interested in a public expression of justice.

I understand the problems of thinking this way, not the least of which is the knowledge that people are simply not that purposeful. You could argue that people often do things in very selfish ways, but they are not driven by a view of God that compels or allows them to act in that manner.

But something does drive each of us, doesn't it? That something can be personal preservation. It can be economic gain. It can be love. It can be hate. It can be fear. But what lies behind *those* values? We believe that beneath those surface values, every person holds a particular view of God and how he would have them act in the world.

The majority of the American church in the twenty-first century preaches a perspective on God that fails to incorporate issues of justice. In this view, God cares for each of us individually and wants to spend eternity with us in heaven. Visit the average American church, suburban or not, on any given Sunday morning. Does the God people are worshiping have concern for those who find themselves in need? Does the God talked about from the pulpit care about the poor and the marginalized? About how we make and spend our money? About how we steward the resources with which we have been entrusted?

We need a new view of God.

Our Story—from Lisa's Perspective

All my life I have known that I should be caring for "the least of these," even though most of my life wasn't spent in such pursuits at all. Yet I had a legacy to live up to for which I'm thankful. My father, grandfather, and uncle were all optometrists down in South Baltimore. When they were in practice, that neighborhood had yet to be gentrified. The everyday citizen of Baltimore lived around Light Street: shopkeepers, longshoremen, and factory workers, to name a few. Many of them couldn't afford the glasses and eye care provided them, but as far as I know, a collection notice never went out from Drs. Ebauer, optometrists. Those gracious men provided for the community in which they worked most of their lives, practicing the profession they had given themselves to, caring for the people around them. The funny stories my dad would tell around the supper table, the people he spoke of, still give me cause to smile decades later.

My father rarely complained about the people who failed to pay their bills. I'm sure there were some who took advantage of the Ebauers' kindness, but that was a small price to pay. The Drs. Ebauer never talked about moving out to a cushy office in the county and charging three times as much for their services. They stayed in South Baltimore until retirement. Though all three men are long gone, they gifted me with the realization that caring for those who find themselves in insurmountable situations is something we all should do as we go about our lives, utilizing the gifts and talents God has given us.

But as typical professionals in the suburbs, Will and I found our lives consumed by the kids' school, sports, church, and, of course, our careers. We had no time to help out others and felt pretty satisfied with infrequent touches of goodness on our part, thinking on that annual night we cooked for the homeless in our area, "Well, at least I helped tonight. How many other Christians do nothing and don't feel bad about it?"

For us, living a life of justice would eventually take forsaking the suburbs altogether and moving into an urban environment. However, we soon realized there must be another way for suburbanites who don't feel called to relocate but care about issues of justice to live out the commands of Jesus in Matthew 25. And so the idea for this book, *Justice in the Burbs*, was born. The fact that you have picked up this book shows that you care and want to use your own hands and feet.

We pray you will find encouragement and inspiration tucked among these pages. If we as Christians don't care to follow the commands of Jesus, who will? Welcome to the journey. There are plenty of others saving you a seat!

Assumptions

Having made several assumptions in writing this book, we'll be very up-front with them.

1. When we say "God," we are referring to the God honored in the Judeo-Christian tradition. We take the old adage "write what you know" to heart. We speak from the Judeo-Christian tradition because that is who we are. While our examples tend to be from people with a similar view, they are not exclusively

from the Christian tradition. Gandhi, for example, had much wisdom from which the Christian church can benefit.

2. Despite point number 1, this book addresses issues of justice that people of all faiths can apply. While we will speak from a particular perspective—followers of Jesus talking primarily to other followers of Jesus—we hope this book is written in a way that invites all to follow along.

3. This is not a how-to book. We hope to provide meaningful dialogue that will encourage people toward a lifestyle of justice. Having said that, we cannot teach you to live justly. We can show you the reasons, give you some principles, and hope that you move toward living a life for others in radical ways.

Book Overview

This book is divided into twelve chapters. Each chapter contains the following elements:

Narrative. All this talk of justice is great, but what does it look like? How does God want us to act? You will follow a fictional family through their journey of questioning and discovery, see their joys and their pains, live through their introduction to following God as a way of justice, and hopefully learn along with them.

I (Lisa) sought to show people we think of as typical suburbanites, Matt and Christine Marshall, as their journey unfolds. While unable to develop character, plot, and themes as I would in a novel, my hope is that within one of these characters you will find a part of yourself, that the questions they ask resonate in your heart, and that their journey will encourage you to make the next step.

Discourse. We desire to give you the reader good reasons to live justly. In addition to the narrative, each chapter contains a specific discussion of related issues. Our goal is to engage you in many different ways and on multiple levels, to allow you to find different entry points for your journey of living justly in the suburbs.

Meditation. We strongly believe that living justly comes as a result of being tied into Scripture and the writings of various people who have been seeking to live out the story of God through the years. We also have some sense that living justly means being a part of the community of God, so we asked some friends to offer their meditations and reflections in response to the story and the ideas presented in this book. Brian McLaren, Christine Pohl, Leonard Sweet, Luci Shaw, and many others were gracious enough to offer us the gift of their words.

1   Life in an Ordinary World

Matt wondered why anybody would give up so much. He pointed to Clifton through the windshield. "I'll bet he finds himself in the craziest places sometimes," he said to his wife, Christine. The wiper blades skated full speed across the beaded surface as they waited at a stoplight. He hated rain.

This congested intersection was a prime example. The man worked this intersection every Friday night for as long as they'd lived in the area—at least four years. Matt admired his staying power. He couldn't imagine begging for money. Well, truthfully, he could. Years ago, he wished his parents would have done so more often. Talk about lean years.

Christine pulled her purse off the floor. "And in this rain. He must be doing something really amazing downtown."

"I'll bet his mission's a rat hole. Clifton must be a saint."

Tweed hair shorn about an inch away from his brown scalp, Clifton elevated a bucket in one large, knobby hand. In red marker the words "Helping Hands Rescue Mission" advertised his purpose, but his charming, easy-chair smile and the way he pointed at people with the question, "You helping out today? Any bit'll do!" advertised his persona. Only the lines around his eyes whispered of his age. A little old school, he made it easy for Matt to imagine him once sauntering down the street as a confident young man. It didn't matter that his shoes looked as if they'd walked back and forth from the mission downtown to this intersection in the suburbs a hundred times or so. It didn't matter that he held a sloppy old sugar bucket up to the windows of shiny motorized toys. Matt suspected Clifton was no fool. He knew the people out here had a little extra money, and he planned to get at least a few of them to help the people at Helping Hands. He'd become rather a folk figure on this humming corner.

On Friday nights, usually the most profitable for him, people celebrated the paycheck in their pocket, ready for a steak dinner and the latest release down at the multiplex. At least that was Matt and Christine's plan. Date nights were sacred for the couple. Three kids made it a necessity.

Christine dug into her purse. "It's got to be hard. That mission's the last stop on the line for a lot of people. They feed a ton of people."

"How do you know?"

"I looked them up on the Internet awhile ago."

"Figures." Matt squeezed her leg. Christine was always looking up stuff on the Internet. Talk about a font of information! He kept telling her such curiosity would land her in trouble someday, but he loved that about her. "I'll bet most of them don't even appreciate it."

Christine faced him, brow knit. "I don't think that's why the volunteers are there. Maybe they just want to help and get the heavenly reward."

"They're better people than I am."

She pointed at Clifton. "Well, look at the man. The rain's practically drowning him, and there he stands. I'll bet that bucket's filled more with water than it is money."

Clifton approached their SUV. "Good evening, fine folks!"

"Hey, Clifton!" Matt waved, then turned to Christine. "Can you get out some cash, babe?"

She leaned over toward her husband's window and waved too. "Hi, Clifton!"

"Hey there." He hesitated, then smiled with a shake of his head. "What are your alls' names again?"

"I'm Matt and this is my wife, Christine."

"Sorry about that."

"Oh, please. Don't apologize. I'm horrible with names." Christine dug through her purse. "I'm sure you've got enough on your mind. Oh, shoot, the light's about to turn." She ravaged some buried compartment. Matt called her purse Mary Poppins's bag. "Here!" She shoved a bank envelope into Matt's hand.

Matt dropped the bills into the bucket. A couple of twenties and some ones fluttered down to rest upon the meager offerings. A lot of water in there too, just as Christine had predicted. Clifton peered into the vehicle with a grin. "Well, you just made my night a lot shorter."

"Good," Matt said.

"God bless!" Christine said.

Clifton shouted as he walked away, "Oh, God does! God really does!"

They pulled away, flowing with the traffic around them, engulfed in a stream of cars very much like their own.

❒

Matt pulled into a parking space at Burger King and turned to Christine as he slid the gearshift into park. "Well, there went our date money. How much do you have left?"

Christine slid out her wallet and slipped a thumb in the billfold. "Five bucks. How about you?"

Matt lifted himself off the seat and removed his billfold from his back pocket. "Six and some change."

"How about we split a Whopper meal and then go to Starbucks?"

Matt shook his head with a laugh. "Feels like college days again. I don't know if the old digestive system can take a meal like that. But I'm willing to give it a shot."

"Yeah, but I can bet you if we walked into Clifton's mission with bagfuls of Whoppers and trays of cappuccinos, the people wouldn't know what happened."

"I'm sure they get good meals there."

Christine shrugged. "How should I know?"

"Yeah, me either. We should drive down there sometime."

"Like we have time."

"I'm sure we can figure something out, can't we?" He could read Christine's thoughts by the look she shot him. *With the hours you work? With all the lessons and activities? With church?*

"Yeah, the plate's pretty full," he said.

Matt wondered if they were eating gourmet off that plate. Or was it junk food, like the Whopper about to be consumed? And no matter how much béarnaise sauce they spooned on it, it would always be a Whopper. "Did your church talk much about places like Helping Hands when you were growing up?"

"Not hardly. Hey, you know what? It's probably good it worked out this way. We're hosting the men's prayer breakfast tomorrow morning. I've got to make up the casseroles tonight anyway and I don't want to get home too late."

"So you've got the lacrosse run for Toby?"

"Shoot." Christine looked up at the ceiling of the car and blew her bangs out of her eyes. "Yeah, I guess I'll have to. Will you be done with the breakfast by eleven so I can take Mom to lunch?"

"I hope so. It starts at seven."

"Yeah, but when Joe gets going . . ."

They slid out of the car, raising umbrellas as they shut their doors.

"Do you think Clifton worries about all this stuff?" Matt asked.

Christine waited as Matt pushed the power-lock button on his key ring. "Nope. I have a feeling his life is a whole lot less complicated but a whole lot more powerful."

"Yeah, me too."

Matt stared at the car parked next to theirs, a flummoxed old black Cadillac wearing a rusty overcoat and bald rubber shoes. Christine was probably right. Less complicated. More powerful. Like that could ever happen to them, since they were seemingly destined to live lives of busy insignificance. Not counting the kids, of course.

He took his wife's hand as they walked toward the building that looked pretty much like every other Burger King on the planet.

"Why does Clifton care so much and we don't, babe?" He yanked open the glass door and she walked inside.

"Because it's important to him."

"Ouch."

"Just being honest."

"Well, you are that, Chris."

Boy, was she. With the way he grew up, living hand to mouth, honestly resenting his parents for choosing obedience over riches, he didn't know how he'd forgotten what it felt like to live in such want. Four years Clifton had stood on that corner. Four years.

"At least we don't just drive on by," he muttered.

Christine shot him a look and greeted the attendant at the counter.

WHY READ A BOOK ABOUT JUSTICE?

When Lisa and I began talking about this idea, one advisor said a book about living justly in the world sounded like a book about eating your vegetables. We all know consuming raw carrots and spinach is important, but who wants to be reminded? Yuck.

Let's stop and get wings instead.

As each of us moves into adulthood, we make choices that shape our lives. We pick colleges, spouses, careers, churches, and homes; we make big decisions. We also make a series of small choices with less significant short-term consequences, like what to eat for lunch, whether to go exercise, and yes, whether or not to eat our vegetables. So with Mom not around to remind us, maybe the broccoli never gets eaten, or maybe we don't even buy it in the first place. Hey, it's a free country.

But we know we need to eat vegetables, right? Those of us who have crossed the magic 4-0 mark are acutely aware of how our diet affects our lives, if not by looking at the scale, then by feeling the heartburn! We wish fast food would live up to its name at three o'clock in the morning. Sometimes even that's not enough to make the change. Maybe we groan a bit in the morning, our backs hurt, our waists expand; but by lunchtime that burger or slice of pizza seems a far more interesting option than a salad.

In the same way, most of us sense some element is missing in our lives. Sometimes we are acutely aware of this. We groan with the world and wonder why everything aches so profoundly, why we feel so far from who we know we could be, from the Garden of Eden, from God. We suspect the missing element may involve how we live in the world and the impact of our behavior. We suspect the question of whether there is justice in the world relates to choices we have made, are making, and will make. But perhaps we have forgotten, or perhaps we never knew, what a life lived justly might look like. The question rarely comes up in regular conversation, any more than discussions about the consumption of broccoli abound at our kids' soccer games.

So we stumble through life with unanswered and sometimes unvoiced questions, some X factor missing from our lives, but we fail to remember or just don't know what that factor is. Or we realize exactly what's missing but have no idea how to incorporate issues of justice into our lives, particularly in a way that would safeguard us against completely disrupting our everyday existence.

We do not like disruptions.

Has anybody pulled out in traffic right in front of you recently? Did the worker at the drive-through forget to include the ketchup? Is your favorite shortcut barricaded by a roadwork sign, forcing you to detour? Then you know what we mean.

We live in a disruption-avoidance culture. Whole industries exist to make life less discombobulated. Grocery shopping too much of a hassle? Order online and we'll have your order ready for pickup. Too busy to get your car washed? We'll come to the office, and if you give us your credit card number over the phone, you won't even know we were there. What's next? Drive-through MRIs?

Why are we so afraid of disruptions? What are we doing that is so completely important we cannot be interrupted?

How we answer these questions affects how we interact with those in need and whether or not we actually live a life of justice. Do we even see the issues at hand? Or, as we may suspect, is the disruption-avoidance team winning and keeping us from asking meaningful questions—how we spend our money, how we use our time, how we raise our children, how we interact with God—that influence whether we live justly on this planet and in our communities?

What Is This Word You Keep Using?

It wouldn't be a stretch to say our family has watched *The Princess Bride* over fifty times. Throughout the film, the bad guy, Vizzini, repeatedly uses the word *inconceivable* in situations clearly, well, conceivable. After one such use, his sidekick Inigo Montoya challenges him with our favorite quote from the movie: "You keep using that word. I do not think it means what you think it means."

What do you think of when you hear the word *justice*? Perhaps you think of a criminal getting what he or she deserves. It is possible this word conjures aging hippies, the ACLU, peace signs, sit-ins, and miles of tie-dye. This word, so infused with cultural and political implications for American Christians—both positive and negative depending on your background—automatically raises hackles. But we desire the church to come to a more holistic and biblical understanding of the word, an understanding more connected to the heartbeat of God.

We use the word *justice* often on the pages of this book. What does it mean? Or better yet, what do we mean when we use it?

We define *justice* simply as acting right in our relationships, as determining how we stand in relation to others in our world. We desire, based on many deeper beliefs about the world and our role in it, to be always moving toward some point where our actions and our hopes for the world mirror one another. While we recognize that may never happen in our lifetime, this is our strongest belief about the future.

Yet we realize the conversation about justice can be difficult when we utilize words infused with so much and such varied meaning. For example, let's consider the word *hope*. Lisa and I might agree on the dictionary definition of the word as "to look forward to with confidence or expectation." Yet if you were to ask us *what* we hoped for, we would talk about different outcomes, quickly revealing that while we might define *hope* with the same basic meaning, our use of it varies. This is from two people who (1) have been married for nineteen years and are raising a family together, (2) worship together, and (3) come from the same basic faith tradition (i.e., conservative and Protestant). Ultimately, while we share the same basic framework for seeing the world, our usages of the word *hope* sometimes part company.

Perhaps some synonyms for the word *justice* might help. While this may not bring us to a precise definition, these similar words and phrases might shed some light on how we define this word. When we think of justice, we think of concepts such as *mercy, compassion, being fair*, and *living by the Golden Rule*. We think of people like Mother Teresa, William Wilberforce, and Martin Luther King Jr.

But Is It Still Possible to Live That Way?

Most of us, particularly if we come from a faith tradition, sense these concepts—mercy, compassion, being fair, and living by the Golden Rule—are important for every human to embody. Many of us, however, accepted a myth of contemporary culture that relegates virtues such as these to forgotten values of a bygone era when neighbors still borrowed a cup of sugar, Sunday dinner was eaten around a large table with family and friends, and nobody would dream of missing church.

Americans tend to live with a Norman Rockwell view of the past. Rockwell was an illustrator who captured views of American life mostly through his work for *The Saturday Evening Post*. His *Freedom of Worship* depicted a group of people of differing races and ethnicities praying together. This famous illustration was done during World War II and conveyed a notion of religious values critical to Americans. At the time, people in this country were looking for something traditional to hold on to as a global war turned their world upside down, and works like Rockwell's offered that. His works are still treasured by many Americans as a picture of what could be if we all had a little more character, a little more discipline, a little more gratitude.

Many Americans today view the past as shaped by images like Rockwell's, images that allow us to hold on to a myth that there was an idyllic time in our world when everyone prayed, cared for their neighbor, and went to church on Sunday. In the name of morality, many today cling to and perpetuate the belief that if we could return to the past, everything would be good and the world would be just.

We do not agree.

In fact, this way of thinking may be harming our efforts to act more justly in the world today. We wonder if an overly simplistic reading of history stops us from living today in light of what we hope the future to be. Perhaps an overly romantic view of the past of America and other Western nations keeps us from seeing the struggles that humanity has always faced in seeking to live justly.

It seems to us that in order to accept the notion that mercy, compassion, and fairness are the bygone values of a former day, one needs an unrealistically optimistic view of the past. Combine this with a pessimistic view of the future that is also distorted, and you have a formula for sitting on your hands and worrying, telling yourself that things will never be the way they were "back then." Even Christ's words, "You always have the poor with you" (Matt. 26:11), are misconstrued as an invitation to do nothing because, some may claim, there have always been poor people, so what hope could we possibly have of doing anything about poverty?

We doubt that's what Jesus meant. Those words about the constant presence of the poor were delivered in between sections of Matthew's Gospel that describe the betrayal of Christ and the march to the cross. Rather than being seen as a statement that there is no hope, those words may be better understood as helping set the context for the work of Christ on the cross, which forms the basis for what Peter called "the hope that is in you" (1 Peter 3:15).

But Hasn't the World Always Been Unjust?

We have yet to realize the hope Peter talks about. The poor really are, in fact, with us. Even the work of Norman Rockwell highlighted the inequities of our recent past. Consider his poignant painting *The Problem We All Live With*, which dealt with the physical danger African American children faced in simply trying to go to school at the beginning of desegregation.

Perhaps this is why the model of Christ is so important. Humankind seems to have some general sense of the need for mercy, compassion, being fair, and living by the Golden Rule. We see hopeful glimpses of this from time to time, such as the scores of people reaching out to help victims of the 2004 tsunami or Hurricane Katrina. But apart from some future hope, these brief looks are merely distractions from the awful state we find ourselves in and the horrible future we seem destined for. Without the lens of a future hope, we would all see the world as existing on a steady stream downward.

In many ways, the struggle for justice can be seen as one of the defining issues of humanity, one important framework for understanding all of history. The public record of this planet tells a tale of people living in relation to their fellow citizens, sometimes well and sometimes poorly. It tells how nations lived in relation to other nations. More recently, perhaps in the last five hundred to eight hundred years, history tells us how well or how poorly corporations have lived in relation to their workers, their culture, and the world. This is not a new struggle.

But rather than discourage you, let this increase your interest in these concerns. The fact that humanity has always struggled with them should provide you courage and confidence in knowing you are part of an epic journey, one that has been the subject of struggles throughout the ages.

In the next chapter and beyond, we will address how our faith impacts living justly. For those of us from the Christian tradition, we have reason for delight and trepidation. We delight in the sense that the Bible and church history are certainly full of struggles for justice, and we can rely on storylines from both to inform us how to act. We have trepidation because, ironically, the Bible and church history are also full of stories of individuals and cultures who acted horribly in regard to living justly in the world, and we know the depths to which we can fall.

But before we turn to faith traditions, can we agree that the world has struggled with issues of justice as long as there has been recorded history? We are not breaking new territory here. So many other cultures, including those with deep conceptions of God and those with none, have sought to address these issues.

You are not alone. By engaging with this concern, you place yourself in the broad stream of the world's struggles. Welcome.

MEDITATION BY BRIAN MCLAREN

The English language is beautiful, but we have a peculiar problem in English. In Spanish, French, Italian, and most other human languages, the New Testament word *dikaios* is always translated "justice," a sturdy and social word that evokes fairness, integrity, right treatment, and equity in human relationships. But in English, translators often choose to translate *dikaios* as the word "righteousness." This is unfortunate, even tragic, because many people hear the word "righteousness" and think only of personal and private "piety" or "religiosity" or "personal morality." As important as these things are, they are not *dikaios*.

So may I suggest that when you read your English Bible, you try to rediscover the word "justice" and let it enrich your understanding of God and the Christian life? Perhaps if you do, this creed will become an important affirmation of your faith.

A Justice Creed

We believe that God is just and that God loves
  justice.
God delights in just laws and rejoices in just people.
God liberates those who are oppressed by injustice
And is grieved by unjust people and the unjust systems they create and sustain.
God blesses those who hunger and thirst for justice,
And God's kingdom belongs to those willing to be
  persecuted for the sake of justice.
To God, justice is a weighty thing that can never be
  ignored.
We believe that Jesus came to display the justice of
  God,
In word and deed, in life, death, and resurrection.
The justice God desires, which he taught, must surpass that of the hypocrites,
For the justice of God is a compassionate justice,
Rich in mercy and abounding in love for the last, the
  least, the lost, and the excluded.
On his cross, Jesus drew the injustice of humanity
  into the light,

And there the heartless injustice of human empire
met
The reconciling justice of the kingdom of God.
The resurrection of Jesus proclaims that the true
justice of God,
Naked, vulnerable, and scarred by abuse, is
stronger
Than the violent injustice of humanity, armed with
weapons, conceit, deceit, and lies.
We believe that the Holy Spirit is here now,
Convicting the world of sin and injustice,
Warning that God's judgment will come on all that is
unjust.
We believe that the kingdom of God is not a matter
of superficial things
But is justice, peace, and joy in the Holy Spirit.
Empowered by the Spirit, then, we seek God's king-
dom and we seek God's justice,
For the world as it is has not yet become the world
as God desires it to be.
And so we live and work and pray,
Until justice rolls down like water,
Until justice flows like a never-ending stream.
For we believe that God is just, and the true and liv-
ing God loves justice.
Amen.

2 HEARING THE VOICE OF JUSTICE

The image of Clifton, rain dripping off his slicker, smile on his face, gnawed at Christine all weekend. Surely Friday nights were the least of his worries. He must buckle under the heartache and pain he dealt with all week long.

Christine had hopped on the Internet just that morning. Clifton was the director of Helping Hands. His grandparents had started the mission during the depression. Must have become a family affair. When she told Matt, he said, "That makes sense. It's all he's ever known. Imagine leaving a life like ours. He was raised around this."

"Yeah, but compared to the people in his neighborhood, Clifton's probably sitting pretty."

"I guess it's all relative, then."

She read him the quote at the top of the website, the words of William Booth, founder of the Salvation Army:

> While women weep, as they do now, I'll fight; while children go hungry, as they do now, I'll fight; while men go to prison, in and out, in and out, as they do now, I'll fight; while there is a drunkard left, while there is a poor lost girl upon the streets, while there remains one dark soul without the light of God, I'll fight, I'll fight to the very end!

She shut the laptop. "The mission feeds people three times a day, opens the shelter when it's cold out, and provides counseling. It even has housing for families transitioning out of homelessness. I had no idea Clifton did all that. Can you imagine making that kind of a difference?"

"Honestly? No. No, I can't."

But before he left for the office, he laid a hand on her shoulder. "Maybe we really should check it out. See what Clifton's doing down there."

"Really?"

"I don't know. I mean, the man stands on a corner every Friday night basically begging for money. They must help a lot of people. My parents could have used some help like that when I was growing up."

Now, as the autumn sun shone and the smoky smell of falling leaves drifted on the breeze, Christine handed her friend Jenna a large tea and a bag of scones. Situating her coffee into the cup holder at her right elbow, she pulled away from the Starbucks drive-through and the impatient woman in the car behind her.

Jenna headed up the women's ministry; her husband, Randy, organized the men's groups. "Did you ever do a missions trip when you were in high school, Jenna?"

"Once. We went down to someplace in West Virginia, did a Vacation Bible School for the kids while the handier people built a house and fixed a church."

"What was it like?"

"It was good. I remember feeling really great about what we were doing, but the next year, I think I had lacrosse camp or something and my parents were hoping I'd get a scholarship to State, so I went to camp instead."

"Did you get the scholarship?"

"Yeah, four year, full ride. And I haven't played since I graduated eight years ago. You ever go on a missions trip in high school?"

"No. Our church wasn't really into doing stuff like that. We had a big missions budget for overseas, but nothing hands-on. So you're one step ahead of me there."

HEARING THE VOICE OF JUSTICE

Jenna dug up a scone, broke it in half, and handed it to the two younger kids in car seats in the back—her four-year-old, Elizabeth, and Christine's four-year-old, Zach. "So you thinking of going on a missions trip or something?"

Christine pulled into the neighborhood megapark, which held swings, slides, bridges, turrets, musical stations, and a sandbox the size of most people's living rooms. "Matt's been talking about helping down at the Helping Hands Mission."

"Where's that?"

"Downtown. You know that nice man out there with the bucket on Friday at rush hour? It's them."

"I love him!" Jenna opened the car door. "But do you really have time to get involved in all that? You just agreed to lead one of our women's Bible studies."

"Yeah." The one for the grieving. Three years had passed since her younger sister Amy died. Unbelievable. After Amy had failed to meet Christine for their weekly breakfast, Christine had found her, looking like an angel in her bed. Christine offered to lead the group because she needed it so badly herself. Would that ache never end?

"So you really don't have time, do you, Chris?"

"That's the thing. I don't know. It's one more thing. And the kids will only be little for such a short time." At least that's what her mom was always saying. Of course, her mom wasn't the same person anymore either. She worried constantly over Christine and the kids, reminding her that they were all she had left. Christine's dad couldn't take the pressure of a wife clinging to him like a life preserver, demanding to know where he was every minute of the day. Their divorce was finalized a year ago.

Jenna lifted her daughter out of the car seat. "Our children are a mission field too."

"I know. I don't want to squelch Matt's idea, though. And I'd like to do it too. There's so much pain down there."

"What would you do with the kids?"

"Take them, I guess."

"Down there? Oh my gosh, Christine, are you serious? Maybe you'd better pray about this some more."

"And keep my mouth shut around my mother. She'd have a fit if she knew."

"Well, that isn't something you can hide forever, is it?" Jenna placed her daughter in the stroller and headed down the path to the playground.

Christine examined her wristwatch as she reached for Zach's hand. Two o'clock. One hour and Laurel would be home from school. They'd better hurry up and play.

They sat at the edge of the sandbox. Christine dug a shovel, a bucket, and some action figures out of her bag. "So what is church for? Really for?"

"To edify the body." Jenna angled a ball cap onto her head. It matched her sweater. Jenna always looked like she stepped out of a high-end catalog.

"Well, they're sure doing a good job of it, if all churches are like ours. But is that all?"

Jenna turned and squinted beneath the brim of her hat. "Man, this Clifton guy's really gotten under your skin, hasn't he?"

No doubt about that.

❐

Christine slid her purse off the metal folding chair next to her and onto the floor beneath her seat. No sense in saving Matt's seat any longer. Her daughter's band concert had been burping along for the last fifteen minutes. Beginning band at Cresthill Middle School reminded her of fusion jazz without the jazz. Without the fusion acid, for that matter.

Matt said he might be late, calling her from the bay tunnel before she left to drop off the boys at her mom's. He was stuck in a tie-up due to an overturned cement truck, and didn't it figure, the AC on the Expedition went the way of all flesh. *How did people deal with situations like these before cell phones?* Christine wondered. *Were they frequently frightened, or did they wait patiently, worrying only when they absolutely needed to?*

Laurel looked so pretty, sitting in a demure pose with her silver flute, the front of her dark hair pulled back into a sparkly, butterfly barrette. First-chair flute in the crazy quilt of sound. Christine could hear her tones, pure enough for an eleven-year-old who could play only two songs. She hated to admit her own high hopes for the child, picturing her in the symphony orchestra someday.

The younger Marshalls, Toby and Zach, were spending the night at their grandmother's home, probably eating chocolate pudding and M&Ms with a Coke chaser. They'd planned a special evening, just Laurel and her parents, with the concert and a trip to Friendly's for ice cream sundaes afterward.

However, too many people in a hurry, including a cement truck, and their plans once again sat beneath the tonnage of circumstances beyond their control. That was the part of life Christine hated the most. No matter how fast she ran, how straight she shot, how carefully she organized her home and her family, she seemed constantly at the whim of fate.

She felt alone so much of the time. A dead sister. A needy mother. And a husband that worked too hard. All the women's Bible studies in the world wouldn't change this part of her life. She'd tried so hard. Nobody knew, really. She tried to hide the ache, carrying her own load as St. Paul suggested, praying for Jesus to come to her in fresh ways, ways she might understand better than in a workbook with underlines. She knew those workbooks worked for other women. But she needed more. She knew that too.

□

The cartwheeling thump, repeating an all-too-familiar rhythm accompanied by her sinking words, "Oh no, we've got a flat tire," urged Christine onto the shoulder of the expressway. And in a downpour. Why did these emergencies always happen in a downpour?

Wishing some Good Samaritan their way, she turned to Laurel. "Stay in your seat, sweetie." She unbuckled her safety belt, checked for traffic, jumped out, and hurried around to the back of the car to inspect the damage. "Just wonderful."

"Mom?" Laurel called from the window. "Did you remember your cell phone?"

Of course not. Matt would be furious. *We pay thirty bucks a month for that thing, Christine, and you can't remember to take it off the charger?*

Uh, the answer to that would be oh-so-obvious, Mr. Smarty Pants.

With all she had to remember to take with her when leaving the house with an eleven-year-old, a five-year-old, and a four-year-old, could he really expect more? She kept telling Matt they just needed to live in a tin bubble Airstream so they could haul all the necessaries with them wherever they went. It would be easier in the long run than dragging around the lime green backpack the kids called her mommy bag.

A more humiliating name she couldn't imagine. Sounded like something from *Parents* magazine. *Stow all your gear! Be ready for anything! Don't let life take you by surprise!*

But she'd always wanted this life, right? Even in college, she had prayed for a guy like Matt to come along and relieve her of her mother's expectations: to be a well-paid, well-manicured "businesswoman," whatever that was. "I was never given the opportunity to be that, Christine," her mom had said. "Stuck in a mold from the beginning."

Only one time did Christine bring up the thought that maybe she'd like to be a social worker. She was nineteen.

"They make no money at all!" her mother said. "Forget it." That ended that. But Matt, driven to succeed, rescued her from being coerced to live out her mother's dreams.

Now as Christine bent down by the wheel, rain poured over her hair, nestled against her scalp, and ran down her face. Just great. The silver dot of an embedded nail protruded slightly from the rubber surface. She looked over her shoulder hopefully. Best to stay in the car until help arrived.

But that night, nobody stopped for Christine. She sat in the car and waited, hazard lights flashing into the darkness, afraid to walk with her daughter along the busy highway to the nearest exit, more afraid to leave her alone. Laurel fell asleep, the radio played soft hits, and nobody pulled over. With no phone to use and afraid to step out and possibly wave down an ax murderer or a rapist, Christine remained in the vehicle, hoping that somebody would take notice of her plight, slow down for a moment or two, and lend a hand.

Surely they saw her there. Didn't they?

She waited. And she remembered Clifton, standing with his bucket at the intersection, asking for help.

ISSUES OF JUSTICE ALL AROUND US

There are many people stranded in many different locations. But hearing their voices may be as simple as choosing to listen to the person in front of us in the checkout line.

Right now, I (Will) am typing these words on a recently purchased Macintosh laptop. I'm sitting at a beautiful antique table found in the resort cabin where I have gone away to write. Already today I have eaten two wholesome meals, breakfast and lunch, and I expect to enjoy a healthy dinner in a few hours when I take a break.

As we think about issues of justice, a key concept is privilege. Many, if not most, of the people reading this book can choose whether we join with justice. This is itself a statement of our privilege. Don't misunderstand me—I'm no Warren Buffett or Donald Trump. Yet I am constantly conscious of how much I have that others even in this country do not possess.

On my way out to the cabin I stopped at a local grocery store. I bought organically grown vegetables and cage-free eggs. Even my snacks were indicative of a person with control over his own life and the privilege to make a wide variety of choices. One of my snacks was baked chips, the type that is not as bad for you but costs more than junky potato chips that leave grease stains on your hands. This was an item I could comfortably afford to buy.

I filed into the express lane and chatted briefly with a college student looking for the candy aisle. I glanced through the *People* magazine edition of "The 100 Most Beautiful People in the World." I looked longingly at the treats beside the cash register, especially the Snickers Cruncher bars, my guilty pleasure.

Slowly I began to realize I had been waiting for quite some time. I had no idea how long. That's when I noticed what was happening ahead of me. A young woman was trying to buy her weekly supply of formula and other necessities for her child. Her first WIC check was sadly lacking. The second check covered the formula, but she still needed two more items. I was drawn into the scene, wondering if she had enough money and what would happen if she didn't. My own fears of being caught short in the checkout line rose in sympathy. She reached in her pocket and pulled out what appeared to be the only money she had at the time—three crinkled dollars—and plunked them down to finish the purchase.

Few of us know how to act in that situation. She was obviously uncomfortable and flustered, her body movements hunched, her expression apologetic. This woman was stranded, and I had absolutely no idea how, or whether, to respond. Should I try to talk to her despite the horribly embarrassed look on her face? Should I look away and risk her thinking I am above speaking to her? As I floundered around in my mind, desperate to know what to do, she threw everything hastily into her shopping cart and dashed out to the parking lot. And this was just the grocery store. What other needs did she have that her now empty pockets could not satisfy?

We often forget how privileged we are. Lisa and I are certainly not wealthy. Our income last year was below the average household income for an American family. Yet we find ways to take trips, buy new clothes, and eat healthy (except for when the Snickers Cruncher proves too tempting).

We are certainly not in poverty, and most likely, neither are you. If you are reading this right now, the greatest likelihood is that if you are poor, it is a condition you have chosen because you've gained different priorities or you're pursuing a degree or art. But being able to decide to give up food, clothing, or other items considered necessities in modern culture for loftier goals is itself an act of privilege.

There are great needs in this world. We see homelessness and poverty. We see people who rely on government assistance to feed their children. We see veterans and the elderly forgotten in institutions. We see deplorable housing conditions. And all this in America, one of the most financially prosperous nations in the world.

Elsewhere people fare far worse. Famine and disease decimate populations, and war tears apart families and cripples or kills children. But if we live normal American suburban lives, the only way we might know about this injustice is by seeing it on a news channel or reading about it on the Internet. Even with the availability of the information and the knowledge of the problem, we often turn away, too tired or sad or helpless to focus on such need. Often we don't even look, focusing on our own heartaches, our own needs.

Justice cries out from so many corners of our society. But unless events break into our lives—events like a man peddling for change on the corner or a picture on TV of a child living in poverty—and force us to ask questions, we often do not notice. Unless our lives are interrupted by an uncommon means, we tend to keep up business as usual.

We need to be interrupted.

This is true in part because it is those very interruptions that cause us to question what we are doing and then possibly reframe our thinking about God's work. Consider Christine from our narrative section. Her church growing up was not "into doing stuff like that," by which she meant missions. What effect does not being "into" caring for the poor and needy have on the kind of Christians we raise?

Life is full of so many pursuits, many of them worthwhile. We get a job, we buy a house, we have kids. This is normal life in the West. Yet frequently the stuff of this normal life so dominates our time and attention that we fail to see issues greater than ourselves. If we are never interrupted, and if we do not intentionally strive to raise people to value the stranger and the needy in the ways God does, everyday activities will crowd out God's call on our lives.

The Bible and Justice

A key concern for Christians in relation to living justly is what we believe the Bible says about this issue. We tend to read Scripture selectively, applying as direct commands those things we agree with and understand, while we outright ignore those elements that make us uncomfortable. For example, we apply the Ten Commandments and the Old Testament ideas about sexuality as rules for living. But why do we not have the same approach when we read commands in Leviticus about relieving debts or providing rest for the land?

What Scripture has to say on the issue of justice could fill a whole book by itself. But allow us to highlight some themes that are repeated in the Bible:

- Care for the poor and oppressed (Luke 4:16–19)
- Concern for the environment (Leviticus 25:1–12)
- God's love for the foreigner (Isaiah 56:5–7)
- Condemnation of those who do not share their wealth (Ezekiel 16:48–50)
- God's view of those who profit at the expense of the poor (Jeremiah 22:13–19)

The simple fact is that the Bible is a story of justice. "But," you might ask, "if Scripture has so much to say about these issues of justice, why have I never read it that way?" Good question. We are often too busy to ask the hard questions of how we can be informed by Scripture in ways that would help us live today. Instead, we approach the Bible seeking to affirm choices we have already made. Throughout history this holy book has been misused, abused, and little more than perused as men and women have searched Scripture for religious means to justify their past, present, or intended future actions.

There is a great line in the movie *Saved* that illustrates this truth. One of the characters has distanced herself from her peers. In seeking to bring her back into the fold, her friends kidnap her, surround her, and hurl Bible verses at her. Unwilling to accept their correction (who would want to be kidnapped and beat up with the Bible?), she turns to run away as one of her kidnappers throws a Bible at her in anger. The character picks up the Bible and says, "This is not a weapon."

The Bible is not a weapon, clearly. But while plenty of modern examples of using the Bible as a weapon exist— in movies, in the newspaper, and on the Internet, for example—you'll find fewer examples as you move back in time.

Consider, for example, the Crusades in the Middle Ages. Rather than reach into the Bible for justification for invading foreign lands, popes tended to create special dispensations. For the first Crusade, Pope Urban II pledged all manner of support for those willing to go and fight against the people he called "infidels." If promised financial gain such as repayment of debt and family rewards such as government protection weren't enticing enough, the spiritual goodies offered, such as allowing participation in the Crusades to substitute for penance and a "go to heaven" card for anyone killed in battle, sealed the deal.

Sounds almost like a promise of virgins waiting at the other side for a suicide bomber, doesn't it?

But the popes did not turn to a page in their Bible, point to a passage of Scripture, and tell the crusaders that yes, indeed, David and Isaiah said this was okay; they didn't claim that the teachings of Paul or Jesus allowed for such activity. It is a relatively recent phenomenon, something occurring over the last five hundred years or so, to think of the Bible as a way to justify bad actions. This would be surprising for those of us raised in today's Christian church, where we hear biblical arguments sallied back and forth on almost every political issue of the day.

Why has Scripture become the weapon of choice for so many discussions in the church? There are a lot of reasons, but we suspect one of the biggest is the way we read the Bible. And where were our beliefs about how to read the Bible formed? Well, you remember the song, don't you? "The B-I-B-L-E, yes, that's the book for me. I stand alone on the Word of God, the B-I-B-L-E." So many of us were trained from an early age to see the Bible as an instruction book. These thoughts were formed with songs in Sunday school and have not changed since. And so, among the many problems with how we read Scripture, one of the greatest is an overly simplistic understanding of what Scripture is and the role it plays in our lives. We move into adulthood with a childish understanding of God's primary written communication to humanity.

This is dangerous. As we grow from children to adults, we mature in all kinds of knowledge. Imagine if, for example, we still believed a few drops of food dye in a cup of water created a magic potion. Or that we could dig to China. We let kids imagine all kinds of possibilities because it is good for their development.

But imagine if we taught raw Scripture to children exactly as it appears. The flannelgraph David would have flannel drops of scarlet blood falling from the bottom of Goliath's severed head. Jacob's sons and their violent raid after the circumcision of the men of Shechem's city might not exactly be a sight for children's eyes, nor would the prostitute cut into twelve pieces and sent to each of the tribes, not to mention the slaughter of Achan's family, Jael and her tent peg, or . . . Well, we don't really need to go on. Our kids are not yet mature enough to handle such stories in their most raw, realistic telling.

Yet as we mature, we must begin to see the Bible for what it is—the story of God's faithfulness to a flawed, rough, often cruel people. Sadly, we often don't teach that to adults. Pastors want to be sure their people keep coming back, and some of the stuff in that book is hardly uplifting. In fact, sometimes it's downright scary! Words like *confusing*, *mysterious*, and *puzzling* come to mind as well.

So most of us engage in a very superficial and reductionist reading of the Bible that allows us to maintain misconceptions, preconceptions, and just plain erroneous ideas. But what if we could remain committed to the Bible yet still be willing to question our conceptions? Bishop N. T. Wright says, "We believe the Bible, so we had better discover all the things in it to which our traditions, including our 'Protestant' or 'evangelical' traditions, which have supposed themselves to be 'biblical' but are demonstrably not, have made us blind."[1]

Why does this blindness set in? Partly because the lens we bring to Scripture often prevents us from seeing the overall story of justice as contained in the Bible. As a result, the Bible is often quoted but rarely understood in its entirety. This makes it easy to pick and choose the verses that we want to use to prove our points or make us feel better. Throughout recent history, a simplistic reading of Scripture has utilized the Bible to justify a lack of care for the poor, the trashing of the planet, discrimination against women, and even slavery.

In other words, some really awful things have been justified by a poor understanding of the purpose of Scripture. The Southern Baptists, for example, used Scripture to defend the owning of slaves. While they have spoken quite publicly against those actions in recent times, it is a good reminder of the many ways we can use the Bible to justify what we want to do.

We need a new view of Scripture.

MEDITATION BY KESTER BREWIN

Edmund Burke is famously supposed to have said, "All that is required for evil to triumph is that good men do nothing." Truth be told, he never actually said this, but even so, the sentiments ring true: justice doesn't simply happen; justice is made.

Justice is a conscious act. We can walk into injustice in our sleep: buying what we like, from who we like; driving whichever car, wherever we like, when we like. Injustice is unconscious. It grows when we sleep comfortably.

I wonder how comfortably Mary and Joseph slept. He was trying to make it as a carpenter—not a great job, but perhaps offering some security. She was just a young girl, with dreams of . . . something.

What were their dreams? Perhaps they weren't far from ours. Getting on in life. Little luxuries. Security in a world of many terrors. Good friends. A place to call their own.

Whatever their dreams were, they were interrupted. Interrupted by God. By a child. Such a tiny thing that turned their hopes and dreams upside down into exile, into pain, into worry and fear and grief. Their comfortable Scripture readings were suddenly made alive, nervous, sentient. Who was this boy? Where was his Father's house?

Evil did not triumph because a good woman did . . . something. And a good man trusted her. Perhaps this is a definition of faithfulness: allowing one's dreams to be interrupted. Faith is opening yourself to the tiny seed of the divine and being prepared to see through the consequences.

Like Mary, we all need to become such "wombs of the divine," to allow some new thing to break through in us, to puncture our comfortable worlds and show us truth incarnate. And like Joseph, we all need to trust those who carry these delicate acts of faith, to nurture them and care for them. For in their interrupted lives lie the very seeds of the divine interruption:

the cosmos tears,
the curtain ruptures,
we have grounds for hope.

3 JUSTICE IN THE BURBS

Matt loved his new shoes. Aldens. He knew he'd get a pair one day. But today was Saturday, and a busy one. The shoes would have to wait until church tomorrow. Matt slid on his sneakers.

Not many people knew it, but Matt and hard times weren't strangers. Growing up as a pastor's kid in a small church that expected two ministers for the price of one and ran his mom ragged, he had wondered how his parents even fed their family on the pittance Dad garnered every week. By the time a pair of shoes made it to Matt's feet, they'd been walking around for almost four years on the feet of his two older brothers. Never the coolest styles for him. He thought every time another pair came his way that someday he would buy any pair of shoes he wanted, price be hanged. But money had to fit in that equation, so he dreamed and worked hard, putting himself through college by whatever legal means necessary.

Christine, the daughter of a dentist, never saw a grueling workday, but she bragged about the fact that Matt sold his plasma twice a week for food money during undergraduate school. Well, at least she wasn't a snob. He had to give her that. And she worked hard now, raising Laurel and the two boys. He took pride in providing for her the life she knew growing up. Not that they were living like some people he knew—those who took exotic trips or owned a sailboat—but he knew how to stretch a dollar, and they never wanted for a thing. Sometimes the credit card inched up a little higher than necessary, but extra hours at the office usually took care of that. The MBA he toiled over before he met Christine was a wise investment.

Matt armed his way into a T-shirt. "Ready, Christine?"

"Almost!" she cried from the kitchen.

Clifton had showed up as usual on his corner the Friday before, so Matt had asked if he had a card. Sure enough, the gentleman flicked it out and presented it to him. Definitely an Office Max job, but it told the tale.

So Matt and Christine scheduled their weekly date for this Saturday morning. They headed downtown. He could see the excitement zinging through his wife as they sipped their coffees and sped down the highway toward the city.

She brought up Clifton and the rain. Again.

They'd had the conversation at least three times, but he didn't remind her of that. Besides, she looked gorgeous when she spoke so passionately. Her dark eyes would glimmer, and she'd keep pushing her bangs away from her forehead with her fingers.

"I'm glad we're doing this," he said.

"Me too," she said. "My mom had a fit."

First he heard of it.

"She said if we got shot, there she'd be, left with three kids to raise, and on and on and on. And wasn't it enough that God took Amy away from her? Did she have to endure it with me too?"

"Oh man."

"It's horrible. But I can't *not* live my life a certain way because she's scared. I won't. It's been three years. I'm not saying she should be over it, but she can't rule me with guilt like she's been doing."

"Well, we won't be late getting back, at least. We've got to get up early for church anyway."

"That's what I told her."

"I didn't realize she'd be so put out."

"I know. If we were headed to the movies, it would have been another matter. And shoot, crazy things can happen at the movies too."

"Has she seen Clifton at the intersection?"

"Yes! She loves him too. I mean, how could you not? But throwing a few dollars in the bucket and driving downtown to help with the fall cleaning are two different matters altogether." Christine tied a blue bandana in her hair and held her arm up, showing a not-very-impressive muscle.

"Yes, babe, you look like Rosie the Riveter."

She laughed. "I know it's goofy, Matty. But I feel really good about this. You don't know how good."

"I think I kinda do."

◻

Christine gagged as she lifted the lid to the toilet. Just one little toilet at this place, and it looked like it hadn't been cleaned in ages. She'd never been good with smells; when Zach finally decided to do his business on the potty, she actually wanted to throw a celebratory dinner party. She kept waiting for what other mothers always said would happen: "You'll get used to it." But she never did.

Matt walked into the tiny room and held out his hand. "Let me, babe."

"Are you sure?"

"Really. I've got it."

She kissed him. At times like this she remembered why she married him in the first place. Matt was the guy who had helped her roommate, a piano major, move into their apartment. He helped move the piano while some of the other guys sat around and drank sodas. That had told her almost everything she needed to know.

Christine walked out into the mission dining room where several people folded up chairs in preparation to thoroughly scrub the floors. She pitched in, wiping them down and stacking them on the chair rack in the corner. They stacked tables, legs hinging neatly beneath the tops, over by the grimy window.

The others disappeared to gather the cleaning supplies, so she took a little breather, wiping her sweaty palms on the sides of her jeans.

A small boy, dark as a raisin, flagged her down from near the door. "Hey, lady, I just cut myself. You all got a Band-Aid?"

Christine looked around. "You mean me?"

"Uh-huh. I was riding my scooter and hit a rock." He held up his arm, a large scrape abrading the tender part under his forearm.

"I've got a Band-Aid in my purse, but you need more than that. Come on over."

She didn't need special training for this! She was made to bind little wounds.

He walked over to her and looked up at her with melting brown eyes. She wanted to scoop him up and kiss his rounded cheeks.

"Let's go into the bathroom and we'll wash that up."

She escorted him to where Matt still worked, kneeling on the floor scrubbing around the toilet. What a man.

"What's your name?"

"Antoine. What's yours?" His voice was scratchy and high yet curious and bold, as if he'd never quite realized he was a little kid in a world full of big people.

"Christine. This is my husband, Matt."

Antoine held two fingers up to his nose and squeezed. "It's nasty in here!"

Matt sat back on his haunches and scrunched his forehead. "Tell me about it."

"You cleanin' this place? Man, you is *brave*!"

By this time, Christine had coaxed a warm stream of water from the faucet Matt had already conquered. "Here you go, just put it under here."

Antoine did. "Ow, lady!"

"Sorry."

"That's okay."

"What brought you by the mission?" Christine tenderly ran her fingers over the abrasion, pushing the fine bits of gravel and dirt away from his damaged skin.

"Aw, they always help me out here when my aunt is working."

"You home alone a lot?" Matt asked.

"Sometimes. I try to stay out of her way even when she is home."

Christine didn't dare ask why.

"Now, my grandmom comes over sometimes and reads me stories."

"How old are you?"

"Five."

She finished cleaning the scrape and dried off his arm with her T-shirt. "I don't think a Band-Aid will do much good. Just let the air get to it."

"Okay." And he zoomed out of the bathroom, through the dining room, and back out onto the street.

By the time they finished, the mission, while not really possessing a glow per se, smelled like it should have. Clifton and his sister Yvette gathered the volunteers for a time of prayer and some of Clifton's special apple cobbler. Yvette raised her arms, getting her praise on and thanking God in a way Christine had never heard before. Her words shimmered, as brightly colored and holy as any stained glass windows that ever punctuated the walls of a church. Her clothing matched the sparkle in the air.

"This is a holy place," Christine whispered to Matt.

"Yeah, it really is."

Her cell phone chirped during cobbler time, and she received an earful of doubt and fear from her mother. "Why aren't you home yet, Chrissie? For goodness' sake!"

But when she climbed into the car, Antoine came running up to show her his arm. He pointed to a middle-aged woman in tight green shorts and an oversized polo shirt sitting on a nearby doorstep. "That's my grandmother."

Christine waved. The lady returned the greeting.

That night Christine tucked Toby into bed, five-year-old Toby Marshall who lived with his mom and dad and was always in the yard when he got a scrape. She sat on his soft comforter, tucked the edge under his pointed chin, and kissed his cheek. Gratitude and sorrow grasped hands and followed her into the bathroom, where she laid her forehead against the mirror and wept.

WE ARE AFRAID

One of the first concerns to address when considering how to live justly relates to fear. Each of us is afraid of the unknown. We are afraid that, like the characters from the narrative, our sheltered suburban existence will be threatened. We may even be asked to clean toilets!

But we are also afraid for our own physical safety. Working in spheres of justice involves going to places we do not know and hanging with people we may not trust. We may have great apprehension about the kind of world that will be created by too much mercy and not enough tough love. We like the idea of criminals being locked away and the homeless taken off our streets.

Fr. Richard Rohr once said, "The opposite of faith is not doubt, it is fear."[2] We seem to understand this at a conscious level. We can read passages about God's protection and intellectually assent to that knowledge. But living it out? Acting boldly in faith in complete confidence that God will protect us? That is something Lisa and I have only begun to act out.

Please do not think we are calling you to live recklessly or without regard to your own safety. Far from it. As we have engaged in various ministries to assist people, we have established clear rules designed to protect ourselves from unnecessary risk. We include this discussion here to give you the comfort that someone understands the fears you are feeling.

We Are Too Busy

In relation to living justly, each of us also has great concern for that resource Americans seem to have in such short supply: *time*.

There is much data to explain why this is the case. But the statistical evidence alone doesn't provide the full answer for this deficit. Even if we could explain the time gap with facts, does it make any sense? In the 1950s, U.S. government experts were predicting that because of increases in technology, the average American would work twenty-three hours a week.[3] So, how's that working out for you?

Why does a nation with so much technology not have the know-how to create a simpler life? Why does a nation that has accumulated so much wealth relative to the rest of the world still grasp for more? We're always astounded when we drive through the parking lot at our daughter's high school. BMWs, Mercedes, top-of-the-line SUVs, and high-end sports cars inhabit the lot. Of course, some family cast-offs are represented as well—those such as Will's first car, an old Checker cab, and Lisa's silver Cordoba with a burgundy landau roof, "opera lights," and peeling paint on the roof and the hood. We're not under the delusion the cars are purchased for the child alone; they're for the convenience of the parents as well. No more carpool! No more pickups! Let's face it, that's mighty hard to resist. Maybe it will finally free up some breathing time.

Americans consistently rank at or near the top in per capita income, yet that money, whether spent on extra cars or convenience foods, cannot buy back the time traded for wealth and convenience. If each of us had more discretion regarding our schedules, we could possibly invest some of the time gained in issues of justice. Lisa and I confess to being nowhere close. Even with the decision to create a simpler, more contemplative life, we feel rushed all the time. We get the kids to school, meet a deadline, buy the groceries, pick the kids up from school, and make sure they are home in time for lessons and homework. Before we know it, dinner is consumed, *Jeopardy!* viewed, and the day gone. And we are certainly not alone.

The average American works about 2,050 hours a year. This puts us slightly ahead of the time worked by a miner in the fourteenth century (1,980 hours per year), and it puts us way ahead of a peasant in the thirteenth century (1,620 hours per year). Some progress. The Organization for Economic Cooperation and Development states that in 2005, American workers ranked seventh in the world in terms of numbers of hours worked per year.[4]

We work too hard, and what do we have to show for it? Stuff. That's the nice word for all those things we have accumulated. We could think of some less nice words, but you get the idea. American consumer spending has risen steadily over the last five years. We are working harder than ever to acquire things we don't need—things that clog up the space in our garage and family rooms and, in some cases, a unit at a storage facility—as well as to clog up our schedules with distractions. Spending on entertainment continues to rise each year; clearly whatever we have gotten so far is not enough.

A friend of ours once complained, "I work hard to make a nice home, and I'm never home to enjoy it."

So we work too many hours for things we don't appreciate. We even play too hard, a bizarre oxymoron of contemporary culture. The catchphrase "I work hard and I play hard" is stated like a badge of honor, and we've yet to figure out what that means. When did sitting down with a book and a cup of tea, doing the crossword puzzle, embroidering, or playing a game of Boggle with the kids become something to disdain? Friends of ours have the right idea. With the release of each new Harry Potter book, they gather the kids each evening and read the book aloud. Those times together will not be forgotten by any of them.

A *New York Times* article in February of 2005 described numerous kids who are burning out with sports-related repetitive stress injuries, sometimes as early as eight years old. A recent radio story offered the same diagnosis for baby boomers, those who are often the parents or grandparents of kids burning out from too many sports.

To paraphrase Mick Jagger, "We can't get no satisfaction," no matter how hard we seem to be trying. We even "church" too hard, some of us spending three nights a week at church-related activities: youth group, prayer meeting, and leadership meetings, to name a few. It seems as though we Americans do all we can to feel busy. In fact, the prevailing answer to the question, "How are you?" is no longer, "Fine, and you?" but "Busy!" This allows us to feel like a player, a bootstrap puller, not a loafer or someone without goals or a to-do list a mile long, not like someone who isn't really going anywhere far.

But does all this activity keep us from thinking about the bigger issues of life?

We Live in the Burbs

The suburbs seem particularly designed to avoid facing the bigger issues of life. It almost feels as if these communities were designed to avoid interruption by anything unpleasant or uncomfortable. Planned developments have ways of controlling who comes near. And electronic garage door openers seal the deal. The number of times we have pushed the button on our car's visor, driven into the garage, and closed the door before we even turned off the engine, we couldn't say.

As we discuss these concepts with friends, there is initially some hesitation, which is followed by resigned agreement. Most of us, at different levels of awareness, understand this nature about the suburbs. The burbs are safe, but they are safe at the price of keeping out questions of need, questions of poverty, questions of insufficiency. In fact, they are designed to maintain an illusion of a particular life, the American dream, where no one is needy, where there is a chicken in every pot and a car in every garage (and a boat, and those tools we never use, and a riding mower . . .).

Let's face it—we don't want to be bothered by those in need. It would be too disruptive. The fact that this is overlooked regularly makes it worth stating clearly. Few of us long to have our daily routine and our normal life stepped into by those who are suffering. Whole industries exist to create pleasurable experiences that divert us from the real pain of life, and their primary targets are middle- to upper-middle-income suburban consumers. If you are reading this book, chances are they are targeting you.

For many years, I (Will) worked in a place that required over three hours of commuting a day, ninety minutes each way. It allowed for a nice life financially speaking, but when I got home at night, the last thing I wanted was to have to care for someone else. My suburb ensured this did not happen. All around me were similar houses populated by similar people. Predominantly white-collar workers. Most in the same income range. Mostly white. Lots of SUVs and Volvo wagons just like ours. If someone not fitting that mold were to enter that space, it would have been very obvious. Not surprisingly, few who did not belong there ever entered that world. In eight years, we never saw someone in physical need roaming the streets of our little development in suburban Maryland.

We felt safer that way. There was no one to harm us, no one to cause us discomfort but the Jehovah's Witness lady (whom Lisa frequently invited in for a cup of tea). But there was also no one to interrupt us. No one to show us an image of God in "the least of these." No one to show us the mystery of a God who becomes incarnated in those whom we care for.

Who wants to witness suffering, poverty, or need? Yet for those who are followers of Jesus, suffering is bound up in the story by which we live. Fr. Richard Rohr once said that Christianity is "the only religion that worships the victim."[5] How quickly we forget that truth and instead seek to obscure suffering, which is often put into our lives to shape us into the image of the one who suffered for the world.

We realize that perhaps you and your family may be dealing with your own issues of sickness, disability, abuse, and loneliness. If you suffer invisibly, you know how hard it is when those who have the power and resources to alleviate your suffering fail to even notice.

We Don't Want to Be a "Liberal"

Next, we come to the dreaded "L" word. We are referring, of course, to the word *liberal*.

This word is tossed out repeatedly as the ultimate insult on conservative talk radio. It is often declared from the pulpit as a decisive theological and sociological insult. In so many parts of the contemporary American church, successfully accusing someone of this most heinous of crimes ends a discussion—case closed, high five, they have no more ground to stand on.

How did this word get so much power?

Questions about liberalism go back a long way in America. The word itself defines someone open to new ideas. And that describes a major struggle in American Christianity.

In the late 1800s and early 1900s, many people questioned the way we read Scripture. Some of their ideas might not seem so radical today. Others would still seem quite extreme even to those of us raised in twentieth- and twenty-first-century American Christianity.

One "liberal" involved in a more open reading of Scripture was a Baptist minister named Walter Rauschenbusch. He coined the now-famous term "the social gospel." Rauschenbusch's reading of Scripture caused him to believe that the kingdom had more to do with forming a particular people of God than it had to do with individual salvation.

Movements by Rauschenbusch and other nineteenth- and early-twentieth-century liberals were countered with what came to be called *fundamentalism*.[6] This group of individuals saw themselves as combating not only the belief systems of liberalism but also the liberals themselves. Liberals, to that school of thinking, became *them*. Those who adhered to the fundamentals could therefore be considered *us*.

The liberal-fundamentalist divide began as a debate among scholars, and its effect can still be felt today. Find out where a seminary stood in relation to this debate before 1950, and you can almost guarantee how that school will approach the liberal question today. You can trace with a high degree of certainty how a graduate of that seminary will feel about someone of the "other" view, even when the person in question may also claim to have some sense of what it means to follow God. As people trained by these pastors and educators, we often likewise have an "us vs. them" lens for other believers. For many of us, "liberal" became an easy boundary marker—a quick way of deciding who was "in" and who was "out."

During Lisa's and my formative years, liberals were definitely "them." They were wild savages from outside our tribe. Anything that came to be branded with the label *liberal* was to be avoided at all costs. In our circles, to say you were interested in promoting "the social gospel" would have been like saying you were in favor of beating up small kittens.

But Rauschenbusch had some good ideas. He understood that the Bible had all manner of things to say about the concern of God for the poor and needy. His willingness to ask questions about the kingdom, God's work in our time, and our role in that work garnered him all kinds of trouble. We suspect that if you are willing to ask the same kinds of questions, you will get in all kinds of trouble too.

This should come as no surprise to followers of Jesus, the one who was branded with all manner of labels, including "friend of sinners" and "a drunk." As we seek to live justly and follow God in the way of Jesus, we must learn to live above the unhelpful labels that divide the church.

We Live in America

But it is not just in the realm of theology that *liberal* is a dirty word for many in the contemporary American church. As recently as 1988, an American presidential election was fought and lost on the merits (or de-merits) of liberalism, with an overwhelming percentage of Christian voters favoring the perceived *conservative* candidate. This political fight, in fact, has been an increasingly energizing force for evangelical voters, with the Republican candidate getting no less than two-thirds of their votes since the 1980 election.

Even broader than our current American political context, however, are the values and ideas we have inherited from a much longer dialogue the church has had about how we live as the people of God in a society. One could trace this question back to Constantine's legalization of Christianity in the fourth century. Before that time, it is believed Christian churches were feeding untold thousands a day. Various ministries met the needs of people. However, since Christianity transitioned from being outside the governmental system to inside, the church has had varying kinds of relationships with the state.

After the 2004 elections, there was much talk about moral-issues voters. This was shorthand in the media for the belief that religious voters identified with a particular conservative message of lowering taxes and banning gay marriage. But is this the Christian message? Is God's agenda that narrow or that defined by a particular party agenda? And if God's agenda does involve reduction in the size of government, are the local congregations that are advocating such action prepared to offer services that clothe and feed the hungry, the way the early church did?

It is good to review our understanding of our role in culture. This has the potential to refocus us on our mission of being God's workers in creation. Some Christians, including Lisa and me, fear that we have lost a distinctly Christian way of living in the world, and we are struggling to regain that way.

For a more in-depth discussion of civic issues, we recommend Richard Cizik's excellent piece "For the Health of the Nation: An Evangelical Call to Civic Responsibility." It can be obtained at www.nae.net/images/civic_responsibility2.pdf.

MEDITATION   BY TONY JONES

Julie, our three kids, and I just moved, and you might say that we moved deeper into the suburbs. In fact, a friend came over to see our new house, and she exclaimed, "This is really the suburbs!" The frightening part of her proclamation is that both our old house and our current house are, by any standard, in the burbs.

So we are confronted with the very dilemma that Will and Lisa have laid out in this chapter, and to be honest, it stings. Too easily we console ourselves by the fact that we surely make less money than those who live on our block, that I work for a nonprofit organization, that we go to a church in the city that's populated by young people with tattoos. But the truth is, those factors ease my conscience about as much as the picture of our Peruvian sponsor child on the fridge.

The good news is that even suburban Christians are getting hip to justice issues. Visit my local megachurch and you'll hear them talking not about building a bigger parking lot but about how they can combat AIDS in Africa. Conservative evangelicals are worrying less about that dirty "L" word and speaking out on behalf of the environment and the poor and the oppressed—issues that have traditionally been linked to the "liberal" social gospel churches.

In my work with Emergent Village, I meet a lot of folks every year who are endeavoring to plant churches. Many of them mention that they want to plant a "second chapter of Acts church," ostensibly referring to Acts 2:42–47, which recounts the idyllic post-Pentecost days filled with singing and the sharing of possessions and food.

What these well-intentioned church planters sometimes overlook is that within a couple of chapters, Ananias and Sapphira are zapped by God for withholding some of their wealth from the community, and the church is never the same. In fact, it seems that the big, celebratory agape meal that was celebrated every week in the early church got trimmed down to bread-and-wine communion because the discrepancies in what people brought to the potluck became contentious.

My point is that even in the Bible we find testimony to the difficulty of living justly in community. Whether it be deeply in the burbs with Julie and me, in the thick of intentional community with Lisa and Will, or in Zambia with my friends Molly and Jeff, living justly with others is hard.

So please don't take this, my theological/meditational point, as trite. It's not meant to be trite; it's meant to be a cry of desperation. My only hope of living justly in the burbs is complete reliance upon God's Holy Spirit. And honestly, I have enough confidence in the Spirit to believe she will guide me into living more justly, because she lives in the burbs with me.

~4 FINDING GOD AT STARBUCKS

Matt lined up the shot. Nine ball in the side pocket. It rolled in exactly according to plan. He stood up straight and leaned on his pool cue. "That's the thing, Randy. It just tore her up inside."

"I don't know why that's a surprise, Matt. Christine's got a heart of gold."

"I fell in love with her because she loved kids so much."

Randy leaned over to place his shot. Six ball, corner pocket. Not an easy shot, but Randy was a better pool player than Matt. A perfect ricochet off the side, and the cue ball tapped it into the pocket.

"Good shot."

"Thanks. Want a Coke?"

"Sure."

Behind the built-in bar, Randy pulled a couple of cans from the small refrigerator Jenna always kept fully stocked. Their work with the men's and women's groups at church meant they were always entertaining.

Randy popped the tabs and handed one to Matt. "So what's next? Obviously Christine's not going to be content to do anything other than jump in somewhere."

"She did some research. There are about two hundred kids in the western part of the county who have no access to a hot breakfast."

"Where are their parents?" Randy swigged his drink.

"Same place Antoine's are, I guess."

"Probably."

Matt parked on a barstool. "So she scheduled that planning meeting at church and made those announcements from the pulpit the two Sundays before it, and only one person showed up."

"I must have missed the announcement."

Matt hated even talking about this, but Randy was the head of the men's ministry. Wasn't he supposed to listen to this sort of thing? He didn't know who else to talk to. His own parents sure didn't deserve that kind of burden. They had retired last year from the ministry and were barely scraping by. Matt had tried to convince them to come live with them, but so far they balked at the suggestion. "Yeah, so anyway, she's a little disillusioned."

"Everybody's so strapped these days, I guess. We've got a lot going on. I'm sure somebody'll step up to the plate eventually."

Matt wished he could feel such optimism. If anybody knew how hard it was to commit to something extra, he did. Everyone he knew was already running around like crazy.

Randy picked up his cue. "Hey, tell me about that job promotion you were talking about at the prayer breakfast. Did you get it?"

Regional manager. He'd been positioning himself for this for several years now. "I got it. I move to the offices upstairs in three weeks."

"Congratulations!" Randy seemed genuinely delighted. Matt liked that about him. He rejoiced in everybody's successes.

"We'll see." He shrugged. "Who knows what the real expectations of the company will be? I've got mixed emotions about it."

"No doubt. I'd say you're doing great."

The conversation followed Matt home and hung around like a stray dog the rest of the week. He watched himself go about his days. Smash the snooze on the alarm . . . grab some toast . . . stop for coffee . . . commute . . . work . . . commute . . . home . . . lessons . . . church activities. That was the only difference between himself and the rest of the guys at work. Going to church and doing stuff there to keep the routine going ad nauseam.

He couldn't remember the last time he'd even picked up his Bible. There it lay on the nightstand, his name in faint gold letters, the high school graduation gift from his parents.

Picking it up from his nightstand, he thumbed through the slick pages, breathing in the familiar smell of paper and leather and ink. He climbed into bed. With Thanksgiving tomorrow, it shouldn't be hard to spend a little time with God, but all he could think about was his earlier conversation with Christine. He had watched his wife grow a little more bitter with each day she tried to get the breakfast ministry going. There had to be something more appealing she could start, something that didn't require people to get up at five a.m.

Christine crawled into bed. The house was full of the warm, sweet aroma from the pies she had made that day, and Christine made fantastic pies. When she laid her head on his chest, his hand automatically found her hair. He loved her scent. Tonight she smelled like apples and cinnamon. And toothpaste.

"I'm giving up the hot breakfast thing," she said.

"Oh, babe. Are you sure?" He thought it for the best, but he wouldn't say so. She was already discouraged.

"I can't do it alone. I just can't."

"No. It's not your fault. Stuff like that takes manpower and time."

"And who has that anymore? I wish Helping Hands wasn't so far away. I'd go there all the time."

"Twice a month is a good start, and Antoine's in love with you, so you must be doing something right. Isn't there anything up here?"

"I guess I could be a Big Sister or something."

"Beginning a hot breakfast program is huge, babe. Maybe you just need to start smaller."

She wrapped her arms around him. "Maybe I had delusions of grandeur or something."

"Nah. You've just got a really big heart. You saw a need and wanted to tackle it. I've always admired that about you."

"Really, Matty?"

"Yes, Christine. You're an amazing woman." He really believed it. Sometimes he wondered why she even married him, some poor pastor's kid who was forced to work hard for everything he ever owned.

She lifted up her head. "You know, St. John's Episcopal is starting a Habitat for Humanity house next weekend. Want me to sign you up?"

"Sure. Why not? I'm pretty handy with a hammer and saw." Maybe he could resurrect some of those construction skills he learned in college.

An hour later Matt lay in the darkness, listening to his wife's even breathing. He didn't foresee this—Christine as the champion, pulling him along for the ride. But it was good.

❏

Matt never knew Episcopalians could be so much fun. And they weren't the only denomination represented. He met some guys from the Lutheran church down the street and First Presbyterian too. And the United Methodists claimed their rightful place in the lineup. He'd always heard that Wesley deemed good works important, so no surprise there.

A guy in overalls and a CAT ball cap strode over, handed him a hammer, and slapped him on the back with the force of a wrecking ball. "I'm Jack. You afraid of heights?" He scratched the side of his nose.

"Not one bit."

"Have roofing experience?"

"Yep."

"Then let's get on up there."

At the lunch break, they gathered in the backyard. A man named Fred from the Unitarian church towed in his giant smoker and served them all the best pit beef sandwiches Matt had ever eaten. All the fixings—mayo, horseradish, barbecue sauce, and onions that brought tears to your eyes from ten feet away—were lined up along a folding table. The local grocery chain donated a cooler of sodas as well as some chips and institutional brownies iced with chocolate and laden with fall-colored sprinkles. The lady preparing to inhabit the house thanked each person, telling them she would honor their labor and take care of that house like it belonged to the Queen of England, she sure would. A bit brash, maybe, but sweet nonetheless.

Matt took a picture of her with his cell phone as she stood by the cooker with Fred the Unitarian, her bright orange coat and her bleached, lemon-yellow hair combining into a citrus salad with Fred's lime green barn jacket and red sweatpants.

Yep, a colorful group.

He sent the pic to Christine right then.

The woman put an arm around her daughter, a teenage girl dressed in blue jeans and a worn black parka. Not having yet lost her baby fat and blushing at everything her mother said, she hugged her arms closely around her midsection. Matt made a mental note to tell Christine about her. Maybe this girl would want a big sister like his wife. Who wouldn't, right?

Jack the roofer invited him for a cup of coffee afterward, so they slid into a booth at the local waffle joint.

Matt thanked the waitress as she poured the coffee, then he turned to Jack. "So do you know the story of that lady back at the house?"

"Pretty sad. Abusive husband who ended up in jail. No child support, of course. She and her daughter Britney were in the shelter for a long time while she was trying to get on her feet. Apparently Britney got the worst of the abuse. She really did have to get out of there. Anything more than that, I can't tell you."

"It was good to be there, to do that."

"It's just the beginning for them." He sipped his drink. "Sometimes you wonder who will make it and who won't. But you've got to keep trying."

"I think they'll make it."

Jack lifted his mug. "Let's hope and pray you're right."

Matt told Christine everything as they fired up the grill for dinner despite the thirty-degree weather. Her eyes filled with tears just as he suspected when he mentioned Britney. "Do you think she'd want me? And her mom, would she want me in her daughter's life?"

"I don't know, babe. She works a lot; I know that. It can't hurt to find out."

She shivered, running her hands up and down her arms to warm them. "When do they move in?"

"In two weeks." He laid the chicken breasts over the flame. "But you can call Habitat, and I'll bet they'll put you in touch with her."

□

Is she serious? Christine waited while Jenna pulled her youngest out of the ball pit, patted his bottom, and sent him up the slide at the McDonald's indoor Playland. She sat back down at the table.

"What do you mean, Jenna?"

"Well, first Matt does Habitat, fine. And I think it's great that you're doing the Big Sister thing. Lord knows we need more of that sort of ministry going on these days. But I'm worried about Matt. He's associating with all sorts of people who don't really even believe the gospel."

"What, that Unitarian guy I told you about?"

"Exactly! I mean, they're not even Christians."

"Well, neither is your pool boy, but you talk to him when he comes around."

"That's different, Christine."

Christine tried to think up a response. She wasn't good at confrontation. She hated it with a passion.

Jenna filled in the silence. "It's not a matter of fellowship or service with the pool boy. And what about the Episcopalians? They're ordaining gay people these days! How liberal can you get?"

"What does that have to do with building houses?"

"It just seems . . . I don't know. Should he really be associating with those people?"

"But they're the ones building houses. I couldn't get anybody but you and Matt, Jenna, to even think about starting the hot breakfast ministry."

"I'm just concerned. You don't think he's going to fall into error or anything, do you?"

"Of course not! Matt's stronger spiritually than he's ever been. This winter has been a real time of revival for him. They've built three more houses, you know."

"Well, doing good works and being right with the Lord are two different things."

Okay. "How so?"

"It's all about a personal relationship with Christ, Chris. You know that."

"All about that?"

"Of course. If we add anything to it, it becomes a gospel of works."

Christine pasted on a smile, reached out, and grabbed Jenna's hand. Her friend really was just concerned, and she had to see through all her words and look at her heart. "We're fine. Really, Jenna. If I get worried, you'll be the first one I come to."

"Thanks. I'll hold you to that."

Christine didn't doubt that for a second. Yeah, she could pretend to be all holy and look at her friend's motives, but sometimes Jenna made her want to scream.

To top that off, her mother called on the way home. "Are you going down to that homeless place tomorrow?"

"Yes, Mom, I am."

"Well, I have a doctor appointment, and I need you to take me."

"What happened to your car?"

"Can't a mother want to spend time with her daughter?"

Christine called and made plans with Clifton's sister, Yvette, to volunteer the following day instead. "Sure, honey. We'll take what we can get, whenever we can get it."

WHERE DO I SIGN UP?

Okay. So right about now you're saying, "Enough! I've got it. I'm convinced. Now where do I sign up?" That is a great question.

If you haven't been attuned to issues of living justly, even knowing where to begin is difficult. Think about it this way. Imagine the doorbell rings. You open the door and find someone has left an anonymous present. It's a beautiful, handcrafted guitar, but there's just one problem—you have absolutely no idea how to play. What are you going to do in that situation?

Assuming you actually want to learn how to play and you don't pawn the guitar for a one-month supply of Snickers Cruncher bars, your first step would probably be to find someone who knows how to play and ask him or her to teach you. For those of you who already know how to play the guitar, this was how most of you learned. Maybe you took lessons. Maybe your youth leader taught you how to play. Maybe you listened to Jimmy Page, Jimi Hendrix, or John Denver over and over again until you got the chords and could replicate them. (If it was John Denver, we've got to talk.) But generally you don't just learn guitar without someone else involved.

And you don't learn to live justly by yourself either. Our first suggestion is to begin looking for those already doing works of justice. If you were raised in the American church, this is going to be one of the hardest steps you will take in this journey.

With the varied "self-help" titles on the market, home study programs, and how-to computer software, we seek to be the masters of our fate, setters of goals, and always moving forward. Americans are entrepreneurial. We have a can-do spirit, which might better be described as an I-can-do spirit. We like to start new stuff. Nowhere is this spirit more alive than in the church.

Take a quick survey of the popular books coming from the church over the last forty years, and this trend becomes evident. This is particularly acute in the evangelical church. In our lifetime, we have gone from cell groups to lifestyle evangelism to seeker-sensitive services to postmodern ministries seeking connection to an "ancient-future faith."

Even in the mainline church this spirit is evident, although perhaps not as obvious. Many of the so-called mainline denominations—Episcopal, Methodist, Lutheran, Presbyterian (PCUSA)—began as a reaction against something. Remember, unless you are a practicing Roman Catholic, you are a "protest-ant." And while the evolution of that name had more to do with a burgeoning movement of the spirit threatening people's positions of wealth than it had to do with early reformers' views of their relationship to the church, it is nonetheless true that in the name of Protestantism, American Christians have participated in a massive growth of denominationalism. Presently, depending on which source you trust, somewhere between 5,000 and 25,000 unique strains of Protestant Christianity exist in the United States alone.

This should come as no surprise, given our history. Evangelists like Charles Finney married American pragmatism with the sincere desire for those in the church to see others join them in the way of Jesus. The American church was never the same after that. Consider the following quote from Dr. Michael Pasquarello:

The distinctively American character of Finney's popular, pragmatic program can be seen in his insistence that preaching must always be practical; that whatever cannot be made immediately useful is not preaching the gospel. Yet in his zeal for reaching lost souls, Finney's definition of "useful" and "practical" was increasingly shaped by a form of Biblicism grounded in private judgment and personal experience, a Christian anti-traditionalism that represented liberation from the wisdom of the Christian past.[7]

For many of us, the notion of launching out in some bold new initiative is seen as part of our evangelistic zeal, as part and parcel of doing the work of God. But what if God would have us join work already in progress?

Working in the Kingdom

Consider the parables of Jesus. In Matthew 13:24–43, Jesus tells the story of a field with some good crops and some weeds. Speaking to people who understood at least the basics of farming, when Jesus got to the part about the weeds, the natural reaction of the crowd had to be, "Pull 'em up! Plant good crops in their place." But Jesus, being more than a little subversive, has the landowner in the story leave the weeds in place. Huh?

Later on, in Matthew 20, Jesus tells an equally undermining story. The owner hires some workers to work in the vineyard in the early morning. Around nine o'clock some other guys show up and start working alongside them. The same happens at noon and three o'clock. And they all get paid the same amount. Scandalous.

These and other stories of Jesus tell us the kingdom economy looks different than we might know or have come to believe. Because of our culture, we have an understanding of a kingdom deeply imbedded in return on investment (ROI). Church-growth consulting firms provide charts and statistics showing where and how much investment will be required to "grow" a congregation. For those of us raised in a market-driven church, this model resonates with our conception of how God works. But does it resonate with the model of Christ? Is it what Jesus would do?

"Of course!" someone might exclaim, moving logically down the line in the Matthean parables. "What about the parable of the talents? Didn't Jesus talk about using our resources well?" We thought you would never ask.

Being Good Stewards

Lisa and I once believed it was our job to gin up God's work in the world. But we have begun to see God's work in fresher and more authentic ways, particularly as we read the parables of Jesus with new eyes. God is already at work. This is what the parable of the field presupposes. We don't create the field; we join as workers. Whether you're coming in at nine or noon, the harvest is burgeoning. And the ROI may not work the same as the return on your 401(k).

This is why Matthew 25 is important as we seek a holistic understanding of kingdom values. Why did Matthew follow the parable of the talents with the parable of the sheep and the goats (see Matt. 25:31–46)? Perhaps the answer is this: the ROI for properly tending the resources we have been given is determined by our ability to use those resources among "the least of these." What would be the ultimate outcome of thinking like this?

First, we would not be so careless with what we have. If we saw our stuff—our money, our time, our families, everything we have—as being given for use in the work of

God, we might be more careful with what we acquire and how we use it.

Second, we might use different metrics to define success. How do we define God's blessing on the church today? More people, bigger buildings, better programs. This is quite alluring. Lisa and I ministered at a small church plant for four years. It would have been awesome to have packed out that tiny church building. But what if God is measuring our success by wholly different qualifications? What if success in God's economy is more people being fed, less people dying of AIDS, and families restored after years of religious bickering?

This is a very different understanding of what we should expect to receive from investing in God's economy. Through this lens, we might be more critical of some of the ways we have been living out the story of God and how we are formed as the people of God. But thinking this way is the best answer to the question of where to get started in a life of justice.

We are learning that some people are already doing great things, and the best way for us to invest in the kingdom is to join with them. Lisa works with Kentucky Refugee Ministries, an organization to which our community is deeply connected. Once a week she drives refugees to doctor's appointments; sometimes she makes sure some of their physical needs are met. You could do that, couldn't you?

I (Will) recently volunteered to tutor a student as part of the Carnegie Literacy Center here in Lexington. I give one hour a week helping a middle school student in math. One hour a week is something almost anyone can give.

This change in thinking has required us to move away from the category of "starter." We love to initiate projects. I have formed several companies in my career, and Lisa is a novelist who gets to paint a new set of word pictures with every book. So the idea of joining in with something already in existence has taken some adjustment.

The other adjustment has been thinking of the work of God as coming from someplace other than the church. Kentucky Refugee Ministries employs a good insider buzzword: ministry. But the Carnegie Center—is God at work there?

Perhaps the parable of the field can instruct us all in this regard. When the workers wanted to tear up the weeds, the landowner forbade them, asking instead that they continue their labors. When I taught the "kingdom parables," I (Will) developed a phrase to help us remember the main point of the parable of the weeds: "Who knows where God may be at work?" The best way to answer this question may be this: "God is at work when people act like Jesus."

You want to join in the work of God? Look for signs of Jesus. Look for people who are bringing "good news to the poor," proclaiming "release to the captives and recovery of sight to the blind," those who are helping "to let the oppressed go free" (Luke 4:18 NIV).

Equally important to knowing we are working for the kingdom, that we are—to quote our friend Shane Claiborne—being "the hands and feet of Jesus," is knowing that we are using God's resources well. We will cover more of this later, and our resource section has some great ideas on works of God that you can join.

Seek Justice

Lisa and I realize that the move toward justice can be big. Overwhelming. At these times we all have a tendency toward stasis. We're somewhat like the third worker in the parable of the talents, the one who buried the treasure rather than risk doing the wrong thing. We would rather think more, study more, make sure we have the "right" answer.

That would be the wrong response. More than anything else we could emphasize, we want to be sure that you hear this message loud and clear: do *something*. Seek justice actively.

One of the most famous verses on this issue is Micah 6:8, which states, "He has showed you, O man, what is good. And what does the LORD require of you? To act justly and to love mercy and to walk humbly with your God" (NIV).

Act justly. *Love* mercy. *Walk* humbly. These are actions, visible signs that we are following God's desires. When we focus too much on *thinking* right, we can forget to *do* right in ways that follow after God's heart. This can manifest itself in busyness of conversation, multiple Bible studies a week, and feeling so secure in our rightness that we don't naturally seek areas where we might be lacking. We contend that any notion of thinking right that does not involve acting right was anathema to Jesus. The apostle James said it succinctly: "Faith by itself, if it is not accompanied by action, is dead" (James 2:17 NIV).

How did our beliefs and our actions become two separate expressions of our commitment to God? How can we have one without the other? We've heard horrendous stories of leaders in the church who seem so upstanding on Sundays but go home to abuse their wife and children. Or what about those who praise God in church only to cheat customers and abuse employees in the workplace?

What role does complacency play in this discussion? This is where we should return to the parable of the sheep and the goats. There are consequences to not caring for those at the margins. In light of that parable, we should all be able to see that there will be a judgment, and it will have much to do with how we treated those in need. Did you give a cup of cold water, a hot meal, clothing, a place to stay, a bit of your time to sit and listen to someone who couldn't possibly return the favor?

Matthew 25 reminds us of the high stakes for all followers of Jesus. We tend to think of Jesus only as the shepherd of mercy and compassion, but to the religious leaders of the day he was a prophet and an agitator, always speaking truth no matter how uncomfortable it made others feel. Consider his words, "Depart from me, you who are cursed" (Matt. 25:41 NIV). Hard words indeed. Couldn't Christ have given us at least a *little* wiggle room here, some loophole or escape clause?

But now that you have read this chapter, you carry the obligation of knowledge. Jesus repeatedly talked about those who have "ears to hear" (Mark 4:9 NIV). By virtue of the fact that you have read and understood these words, you have been given "ears to hear." How will you respond?

It's not as daunting as you might think. Nobody expects you to be the next Mother Teresa. We recommend that you start small. Don't think that you need to invent the ultimate justice ministry. Join with those who are already doing the work. But start. Your journey toward justice begins with your next step. Perhaps Jesus lives right next door or down the street. He might even be in your own home.

MEDITATION BY CLAUDIA MAIR BURNEY

Jesus lives next door. He's an eight-year-old girl and her three-year-old brother. The Son of Man looks like those starving Ethiopian children. He only gets breakfast and lunch at school, when he makes it. His mama is a crack whore. Nobody knows where his daddy is. I heard his mama lets her "Johns" do things to him.

Poor King of Kings.

Jesus is two houses down and has six children. Now he's pregnant with the seventh. I don't know if he hasn't figured out what birth control is, or what, but how does he expect his husband to feed all those babies on that salary? And you know with all those kids the Lord of Lords can't work. That

80

means hardworking taxpayers' money has to go for Christ's food stamps!

He needs to get fixed.

The Lord is a crazy man—paranoid schizophrenic. If he doesn't take his medication, he walks up and down the street, cussing and spitting on everybody he passes. He's homeless. Nobody knows where his family is—if he's got one. Digs out of the trash cans for food. Somebody ought to get him off the street.

Jesus is nothing but a nuisance.

I'm starting to see the Son of God everywhere I go. He's always crying or begging or looking pitiful. Why doesn't he pull himself up by his bootstraps? This is America! Makes me mad. He's ruining our neighborhood.

Somebody ought to do something about him.

Somebody.

5 WHY SHOULD I CARE?

Sometimes Christine wished she'd never gotten involved in any of this. She was happier, so much happier, before she realized what a foothold evil had in the world, when she could drive around her neighborhood, admire someone's new car or landscaping, buy her flowers for spring planting, make a trip to Home Depot, and wander the aisles, imagining all the wonderful things she could do with her home as the years went by. And the clincher? She didn't even realize how happy she actually was back then!

Other than her grief about Amy, of course. Amy would have understood these changes in their life. Amy would have cheered them on.

Matt didn't realize she was still working through her sister's death from sudden heart failure. But she could push that grief down when she needed to. She had been trained from a very young age to behave herself.

It was amazing how full and frantic her thought life had become. She thought about people in Africa now dying from AIDS or war, girls exploited in the sex-trafficking industry, widespread starvation, who might need the next Habitat house, and Britney and Antoine. She thought about Antoine a lot, often buying Little Debbie Star Cakes at the grocery store and setting them aside for her trips to Helping Hands. A dollar for a box of those things was easy payment for his hugs and his sweet kisses on her cheeks.

Maybe the trips to Home Depot weren't that important. But still.

She pulled out a loaf of bread and some cheese, set a skillet to heat on the stovetop, and began assembling grilled cheese sandwiches for Toby and Zach, who had looked ready for a nap an hour ago on the way home from women's Bible study. It was all she could do to keep her four-year-old awake in his car seat. Why their ears weren't ringing from that ridiculous kid pop CD Zach decided he wanted for Christmas four months ago remained a mystery.

She felt herself pulling away from her church family, becoming judgmental over their inaction. It wasn't right, she knew, and she hated her feelings. Yet if one person said, "We believe in what you're doing," she knew she'd be back on track. But nobody ever did, even though she and Matt kept up with their church commitments as before, still unable to figure out what to drop.

She slathered butter on the bread.

She was beginning to understand exile.

But truly, the lack of support wasn't the sum of it. It was the burden of knowledge that bowed her back. Christine cursed herself for being an Internet junkie once the kids went down for bed. When she realized the pain that bound the world in iron cords, she could hardly bear the load. What was God doing? Was it like the deists always said, that he created the world, set it in motion, then sat back to see what would happen?

She arranged the sandwiches in the pan.

But she didn't believe that about God, did she? Look at Britney. After a few months as her Big Sister, they were already giggling together over private jokes, and Britney had begun to voice her own agony. There was Jesus in the world if she ever saw him. And Clifton and Yvette, how much Jesus were they? Jack and the other people at Habitat too.

Jesus was all over the place.

"Boys! Go wash up!"

They ran through the kitchen into the bathroom. And that room would be soaked in ten seconds flat.

So why was the world in such a mess?

She flipped the sandwiches over.

I was hungry and you gave me something to eat, thirsty and you gave me something to drink, naked and you clothed me, sick and in prison and you came to me.

But it all seemed so big, so daunting. Satan gained footholds in empty bellies more easily than full ones. It was up to God's people to do the work of God. She just didn't realize the mammoth proportions of the job.

She gently laid the sandwiches on the cutting board and sliced them into four triangles apiece. On two plates she dropped a handful of Fritos and some orange slices. A feast surely.

That night she talked to Matt about it. "I felt so thankful, hon. And those sandwiches really did look like a banquet. I used to ask why I get to live with such abundance while other people starve. And I think God told me because those who are given abundance are given it to share."

"Sounds like something he might say."

❏

Christine slid in her pearl earrings, smoothed her dress. "Do I look all right?"

Matt looked up as he knotted his necktie. "Great. How about me? Is this tie okay?"

"I bought it for you."

"'Cause you know Clifton and his sister are going to be dressed to the nines. He always looks so dapper on Friday nights. At least when it's not raining! Ready?"

"As soon as Britney gets here."

They knew better this time than to ask Christine's mom to babysit. The mission remained a sore spot, more sore than merely fear would aggravate, and they couldn't figure out why until one day she said, "Nobody helped my parents out when we fell on hard times. We had to figure it out on our own."

Well, sure, Matt had thought at the time, *me too. The symbol for my childhood could well be a tuna casserole, but even I can't understand my mother-in-law's begrudging attitude.*

Britney, now settled into her new room at the Habitat house that Christine had helped her decorate, arrived in her typical blue jeans and shyness. She received Christine's careful instructions and immediately sat down with the kids to play a game of Candyland. Matt couldn't have foreseen how Christine's investment in this girl would actually end up coming back to bless them. The kids loved her, and he knew the babysitting money she took home with her would help out her and her mom immensely. They paid her more than they would any other babysitter but chalked it up, tithewise, as one of those matters for the great accountant in the sky.

"Britney, honey," Christine said as she grabbed her purse, "there are snacks in the refrigerator and some dinner leftovers if you're hungry after the kids go down." When she hugged the kids good-bye, Britney got in line. "They'll be fine, Mrs. Marshall. I wouldn't let anybody touch them."

Oh, Lord, Matt thought. He knew where those words came from. When Britney opened up about the abuse of her father last week, Christine cried for two days. Christine cried a lot more than she used to. Matt thought of her tears as a healing salve on the wound of her sister's death.

But tonight she looked simply joyful. They were headed downtown to pick up Clifton and Yvette for a nice dinner at McCormick and Schmick's. He doubted the siblings had many nights on the town. Sure enough, when they arrived the two were ready, dressed in their finest and outshining Matt and Christine. Yvette's orange suit proclaimed their arrival to the restaurant well before they stepped inside.

She picked up her menu, her bracelets jangling and her slick orange fingernails catching the light. "Now, if they have soft crabs, I will have died and gone to heaven. What are you all having?"

Christine always went for the Ahi Tuna, rare, with wasabi; Matt usually ordered whatever unusual happened to be on the specials board: octopus tonight. But Clifton decided that "a crab cake never did anybody any harm."

After they ordered, Clifton laid his hands on the table. "We sure appreciate this little night out. Doesn't happen but once in a blue moon, does it, Yvette?"

"I feel like a real person, not some exile."

"An exile?" Christine picked up her iced tea. "How so?"

Yvette waved a hand. "Oh, being down there day in and day out when I know I could be in some law office somewhere."

"You know she's a lawyer?" Clifton asked.

Matt shook his head. "I didn't."

"My sister takes care of all the legal needs of the mission as well as for our clients. She's a whiz."

"I had no idea," Christine said. "Did you ever do any corporate work?"

Yvette twiddled with a fork. "For a few years, and I was darn good at it. But I couldn't just rake in all that dough and watch Clifton sweating it out down there. He was keeping Grandmom and Grandpop's dream going, and I was having a high time. The guilt was too heavy a burden to bear. So I sold my home, bought a little row house near the mission, and I've been there ever since. Found a nice man too, had a couple of kids, and they're doing well now. Renaul died a few years ago."

"I'm sorry." Christine looked down at her plate.

Yvette set her fork down. "There's heartache all around, Christine. And that's a fact. Some people try to hide from it, but it just can't be done."

"I lost my sister three years ago," she whispered.

"Oh, honey." Yvette laid a hand over Christine's. "So you know what grief feels like."

"I do."

Matt realized something then, the reason Christine was taking to all this like gravy to rice. She knew pain. Maybe he knew want. But she knew pain.

"But what about being an exile?" Matt asked later, just after the waiter arrived with the first course, appetizers to pass around.

Clifton cleared his throat. "It goes back to our African roots. We were taken away, like the children of Israel. And like the children of Israel, we're trying to plant gardens, build houses, raise up our children. I believe it's part of living as the people of God. Unfortunately, it's easy to think we're living in the land of milk and honey. Especially in America."

"Guilty," Matt said.

Clifton lifted up a cracker with crab dip. "So what about you all? Experiencing any exile of your own now that you've stepped on the justice path?"

"Oh yeah." Christine blew upward at her bangs. "From my mom, from some friends. At least Matt's parents have been pretty cool about it. But then, they live in Alabama now."

Clifton sent her a smug smile. "Get used to it. It's threatening to be a role model for the common good."

Matt suppressed a laugh. Role models? Them? Not exactly. "How do you deal with it?"

Yvette wiped her mouth. "I try not to think about it. Right, Clif?"

"You can only do what you can do. Most people, it's just their opinions, and an opinion by itself never did a thing for anybody. I just feel sad because they're missing out on some of the most wonderful blessings God has for his people."

That night when Matt drove Britney back to her new home, and she chattered about the games she played with the children, how she'd organized kickball for the neighborhood kids, and, boy, did his help with her geometry really do the trick for that test, he knew exactly what Clifton meant.

Exile was rewarding. Didn't make it easy, mind you. But it made it worthwhile. What saddened him most was that he knew it was going to get worse. They couldn't go on with this schedule forever. Church, school, and now this stuff. Something had to go.

IT MATTERS TO YOUR WORLD

Ugh. Another thing to care about. Just when you had your schedule down, your job figured out, and time to get the kids to baseball practice. Right about now you are asking, "Do I really need another thing to worry about? Why should I care?"

To begin with, living justly truly matters to our world, whether we like it or not. We talked in the previous chapter about fields and sowers and those who do the work of the kingdom. Many of the present teachings of the church about living justly tend to be rooted in the words of Jesus. But we see this whole subject as having much deeper roots in the overall plan of God. If you have been hanging around a church in America for any length of time, chances are you have heard a sermon on the following passage:

> For surely I know the plans I have for you, says the Lord, plans for your welfare and not for harm, to give you a future with hope. Then when you call upon me and come and pray to me, I will hear you. When you search for me, you will find me; if you seek me with all your heart, I will let you find me, says the Lord, and I will restore your fortunes and gather you from all the nations and all the places where I have driven you, says the Lord,

and I will bring you back to the place from which I sent
you into exile.

Jeremiah 29:11–14

When we hear this passage preached, the focus tends to
be on God's future redemption and restoration. And let's
face it—we all want our fortunes restored. But is this the
whole story? What came before these verses? What led up
to this promise?

Thus says the LORD of hosts, the God of Israel, to all
the exiles whom I have sent into exile from Jerusalem
to Babylon: Build houses and live in them; plant gardens and eat what they produce. Take wives and have
sons and daughters; take wives for your sons, and give
your daughters in marriage, that they may bear sons
and daughters; multiply there, and do not decrease. But
seek the welfare of the city where I have sent you into
exile, and pray to the LORD on its behalf, for in its welfare
you will find your welfare.

Jeremiah 29:4–7

"In its welfare you will find your welfare." God knits
together the future of the city and our actions. While we
tend to focus on the notion of deliverance, it is less exciting to think about living day to day as exiles. We would all
love to escape to that place where goodness and provision
abound.

There is much being written in the church these days
about when the world will end, who gets to be rescued,
and who gets "left behind." Truth is, Lisa and I are a little
suspicious of such talk. Not that we think there is no end
to which we should be anxiously looking. We believe Christ
will return, and that knowledge fills us with great hope. But
we fear for the kind of church and the understanding of
Jesus that is created when there is too much emphasis on
the future and not enough on the present. Jesus said the

day and the hour is not known, and we must occupy while he tarries. Occupy what? Our places of exile. This world. The suburban neighborhoods where we live.

The people of God have always struggled with this problem. Written approximately six hundred years before the birth of Christ, the book of Jeremiah tells of a people who forgot why they were chosen. The people of Judah failed to remember their calling, and God had brought them into exile. They longed to get the heck out of Dodge, or, in this case, Babylon. They longed for God to deliver them.

Jeremiah was handed the depressing job of telling the people that if they wanted any hope of rescue, they needed to learn to live in exile. This explains the importance of the first part of chapter 29. While it's true there was to be a future deliverance, it was predicated on their ability to live in exile. Ironic, certainly, but this theme runs throughout the Old Testament.

This brings us back to the original question: "Why should I care?" Because, when it comes to living justly, to quote Jim Wallis, "We are the ones we've been waiting for."[8] In your hands and feet is the power to influence the world. Jeremiah was conscious of this fact when he explained to God's people that Babylon's future and their future were inextricably linked.

This is a thoroughly biblical notion—the idea of our involvement in God's work. Consider, for example, the Old Testament concept of shalom. When David invoked shalom in his prayer for the peace of Jerusalem, he was not asking merely for the absence of war. The word *shalom* holds more richness and complexity than such a singular definition. David was also asking for the welfare of the city. He was asking for a sense of completeness that comes from individuals acting responsibly. Shalom exists when everyone is doing what he or she is supposed to do. Shalom is not an ethereal concept. It happens on a global scale when individuals take responsibility.

It Matters to the Church

While we believe an understanding of our individual roles in living justly is critical, we think that the ultimate goal of individuals acting justly is communities that do so. The predominant teachings of the Bible, both Old and New Testaments, describe how to live as just people, as shalom people. The closest we can get to these attitudes today is found in the word *community*.

God's concept of world peace has always involved a peaceable community. "Blessed are the peacemakers," Jesus said, referring to a group of people living in radical discipleship to the way of God. But American Christians are so individualistic that they have difficulty seeing the possibility of a global peace that requires each person to play a part. What would it mean to live together as the people of God, seeking peace and justice?

This is the point at which the way of God becomes religious. We believe one of the most misunderstood words in the English language is the word *religion*. Its most recent meaning comes from the Latin verb *religare*, which means "to tie fast together." One might use the verb to describe a bundle of sticks gathered for firewood. They are tied together for a communal purpose. One stick will not let off much heat, cook a stew, or warm a home, but those sticks together can do meaningful work. Similarly, being bound together by *religion* is a critical value for us if we hope to transform our culture.

However, the word *religion* has come to be devalued and scorned. People say things like, "I love Jesus, but I don't like religion." That's a shame, really. Followers of Jesus have always been linked by a common set of values. That is what it means to follow Jesus—to be a people held together by common values, the same values held by Christ himself. Remember what Jesus prayed for: "I ask not only on behalf of these, but also on behalf of those who will believe in me through their word, that they may all be one" (John 17:20–21).

We fully understand that in the name of religion all kinds of atrocities have been committed. We all know about the big ones—the Crusades, "holy" wars, manifest destiny, and so on. But it is the smaller atrocities—sermons preached to achieve political or personal goals, givers who withhold their donations until they get their way, power wielded to create programs that increase attendance while harming a congregation's values—that may have a bigger effect on our world and us.

Take these steps in a culture already predisposed to think individualistically, and the results can be disastrous. Rather than flocking toward the idea of being united by a common set of values, Americans have tended to be deeply suspicious of any religious notions. Instead of committing our hearts and minds to the religious values of the group, we seek to "find ourselves." How does such thinking affect the gospel?

Missionary writer Lesslie Newbigin talked about a congregation being a "hermeneutic of the gospel," a fancy way of saying that how we act as followers of Jesus interprets for the larger culture the "good news" about Jesus. When we act individualistically, when we don't seem to be moving in concert with other followers of Jesus, that becomes a statement to those around us. It's hard to convince the world of the love of God when we have a hard time loving each other. It's hard to convince the world that Jesus cares when we don't.

Nowhere is this more evident than on issues of justice. The church in America seems far more enamored by the governmental process than by the sacrificial act of giving to each other and to a world in need. Judging by our actions, it seems we would rather show up every four years and vote than show up every day to be the agents of God's work in the world. Our actions send a clear message to those in need: "We don't really care about you."

Recently the work of the church, particularly the American evangelical church, has come to be perceived as being more about power and control than about bringing the love of Christ to the world. We have become like a distant parent who says he or she loves the child but shows up only when it's time to discipline him. This has significant impact on the church and the culture's understanding of the gospel. The wonderful story of redemption available by converting to the way of Jesus becomes an empty slogan on the march to political dominance.

It Matters to the Future

That "empty slogan" has a massive impact on the way our culture is formed. We are presently shaping the world our children will live in.

The church in America has been on the forefront of some of the greatest historic struggles for justice. John Wesley, for example, fought adamantly for the rights of workers. He preached sermons and expressed very public statements against employers who paid their workers in moonshine. Today many who attend churches in the tradition of Wesley—United Methodist, Wesleyan, Free Methodist—tend to be teetotalers. This practice can be traced directly to Wesley's campaign.

Though Charles Finney injected American pragmatism into our understanding of the gospel, he was nonetheless a valiant fighter against the injustice of slavery. He joined Englishman William Wilberforce and so many others in speaking for justice on this issue. He was not afraid to call slavery sin, and he preached multiple sermons on the topic, rousing Christians to action.

These men are spoken of highly in regard to their contribution to the church. And because the church and culture are so deeply related, their desire to cause people to act more justly also caused us to have a more just society. In more recent history, we have heard the bold voices of Dorothy Day and Rev. Martin Luther King Jr., individuals who spoke to our religious beliefs, our public practice, and the relationship between the two. In fact, today Americans enjoy so many freedoms because of the direct actions of those within the church that it is hard to imagine life in this country without those freedoms. But let's do that for just a moment.

Let's suppose that American Christians still owned slaves. Can you imagine the outcry from our sisters and brothers in Africa? There are now more Christians on the continent of Africa than there are people living in the United States. Do you believe the gospel would ever have taken hold in Africa if slavery were still legal in America, a nation closely associated with Christianity?

Or imagine you grew up without your parents because they were killed in a work-related accident, since no one had ever bothered to speak in favor of safe working conditions. Imagine if American companies treated our workers the same way that many of the countries we buy our clothes from do. Imagine telling people about the love of Jesus in that type of world.

In relation to living justly, so much is at stake, especially the future we are creating and the question of how the gospel will be accepted in that world. Sometimes we have a tendency to view justice as something we want to do, but it's something we will get to when we have time. The church, the gospel, and the future of our nation depend on how we choose to live.

MEDITATION   BY LEONARD SWEET

Two things define *justice* in a biblical context.
First, there is no understanding without standing under.

Second, the question is not "What are you standing for?" but "Who are you standing with?"

Each is a major paradigm shift from how "justice" ministries are conceived and conducted in the church today, a modern church that was founded on three words spoken by Martin Luther almost five hundred years ago: "Here I stand."

In fact, you could argue that the whole of modern culture was founded on the three words "Here I stand." First, "here." Modernity was all about the "here and now," the existential moment (hence Christian existentialism), and shifting our focus from past to present. Second, "I." Modernity in some ways invented the concept of the individual as we know it today—an autonomous, self-defined, discrete person who is free to choose a multiplicity of identities and "selves." Third, "stand." The modern world focused on an understanding of truth as rational principles and proclamations that led one to "bear witness" by "taking stands," formulating propositions, and passing resolutions.

The problem with all this is that each of these words is wrong for the world we are living in. The time zone of postmodern culture is not the present or the past but the future. It's no longer "here" but "there." The individualism of modern culture needs more focus not on the self but on the community. It's no longer "I" but "we." And we're "standing" so much that it's time to take a hike. It's no longer "stand" but "go." The words postmodern culture needs to hear from the church are not "Here I stand" but "There we go."

The problem with "Here I stand" justice is that in the Bible, love and justice are yoked concepts, and both are personified in a "There we go" Jesus. It is standard exegetical procedure to note that in John's Gospel, wisdom is personified. But the uniqueness of Christianity is that *truth* is personified, and not just in John's Gospel. Truth is personified in the person of Jesus.

Take the apostle Paul, for example. Even though the earliest written words of Jesus in the New Testament come from

Paul ("This is my body. . . . This cup is the new covenant in my blood" [1 Cor. 11:24–25]), only one time does Paul quote Jesus directly, and only four times does Paul reference the words of Jesus (see 1 Cor. 7:10–11; 9:14; 14:37–38; 1 Thess. 4:15–17). In fact, if all we had was Paul, we would know almost nothing of the teachings of Jesus. Paul is not at all interested in quoting the propositions and "stands" of Jesus. What absolutely mesmerized Paul, however, was the person of Jesus and what he did: Jesus was born, he was crucified, he was raised, and he will come again. In contrast to the Gnostic gospels, which are fixated on Jesus's statements and disinterested in the person of Jesus and what he did, for Paul Jesus was a dying and rising and returning Savior. Jesus's "stands" and "statements" also take a backseat to Jesus as the dying and rising and returning Christ in the rest of the biblical letters, including James, Jude, and Peter, and even in the nonepistolary, narrative text of Revelation.

What if the "Christian position" on the hot-button issues of the day is less a statement than a stance, less a principle than a posture? Instead of "What are we standing for?" why aren't we talking about "Who are we standing with?" Isn't it the nature of disciples of Jesus to be known less for a certain opinion about an issue than to be known for who we are in relationship with? Maybe our hot buttons are less about "issues" than about "relationships." Wasn't it Jesus who made the final quiz not one of "What are you standing for?" but one of "Who are you standing with?"

Or, as Jesus put it directly, "Inasmuch as you did it to one of the least of these My brethren, you did it to Me" (Matt. 25:40 NKJV).

6 CAN I ANSWER "TOO BUSY"?

C hristine had to give credit where it was due. The more she researched and saw what the church was doing in international adoptions, the more impressed she became.

"I'm not sure if I'm ready for that yet," she told Matt as they sat on the sidelines of Toby's T-ball game. "But I really admire it."

"Me too, babe."

"And it does give me some hope, you know?"

"Sure. So . . ."

"So I got online . . ."

"Of course."

". . . and I found a school for deaf children in Kenya. It's called Humble Hearts, and, well, so far we haven't invested too much money in this stuff, and there's the cutest little boy named Pascal who doesn't have a sponsor yet, and it's only twenty dollars a month."

"We can sure swing that."

"I know."

"You already signed up, didn't you?"

She nodded. "He'll write letters, and we can send him things. The sponsorship only covers his school fees and uniform, but there's a list of other items we can provide additionally."

"How much?"

"Depends on how far you want to go with it. But honestly, we can cancel the weekend away we were going to have out at the lake and clothe him for the next year, plus provide a backpack, school supplies, and fruit for the whole school that he gets to give out."

"Let's do it."

"I mean, it's easy enough, right?"

"Right."

"And who knows who he'll grow up to become?"

Matt touched her arm. "I said it sounds great, babe."

Christine watched as Matt picked up Zach, threw him in the air, and set him back down. He took his hand and walked him over to the concessions stand. Normally he bought at least four things, but when they returned with just a couple of Airheads, Christine realized these life choices went clear down to the bone.

Toby and Laurel were just as thrilled with Airheads anyway. She was done placing her own bloated expectations on her children, was done having them herself.

□

Truthfully, Matt felt a little disappointed after taking Christine over to Pinewood, a great new development being constructed further up the expressway from town. Due to the promotion, they had more money than ever before. People were snatching up the lots faster than the developers could clear them. It was everything he and Christine had ever dreamed about, and just a mile away from the country club they could finally afford.

But he didn't dare bring it up to Christine. She already complained they had more room than their family could possibly need, and why not let somebody live in the finished basement? "Remember Miss Edith? She's about to go into the county home for the aged. It's got to be terrible for her to lose her little apartment like that."

All those dreams he'd had for so long, she was slowly replacing with something new. How could she stand it?

He'd give her time. Maybe she could see it was possible for them to have it all and still be responsible to their faith. Right? Isn't that what some of those guys on TV said?

When she suggested trading in the SUVs for something more economical, he practically bit his tongue. He loved his Expedition.

And she just laughed, darn her. Oh man. What was next, hand-me-down shoes?

❏

Christine knew the call was coming. Jenna and Randy invited them to dinner. The Marshalls had finally had to cut back on their hours at church. Going down to the mission twice a month, not to mention Matt's involvement with Habitat and Christine's with Britney, was taking its toll on their family. After a month of prayer and laying it all out Matt-style in a spreadsheet, they'd come to the decision their justice works needed them more than church did. They'd still teach Laurel's Sunday school class. That was nonnegotiable.

But that left youth group, the men's prayer breakfast, the women's Bible study group, and the grounds crew without their help. Leadership meetings every other week were a killer too.

"We were overinvolved anyway," Christine said as she loaded the kids in the car to head over to Randy and Jenna's. "Surely they can see that, Matt."

"I don't know. It's so fast-paced these days, I think everybody really believes if you're not doing something major with every waking minute, you're a bad steward of your time. We did."

"Notwithstanding the fact that even Jesus took time away."

"Hey, you don't have to convince me."

DO I HAVE TO ANSWER?

"Can't I just answer 'too busy'?" you say. Just by virtue of the fact that you're reading this, you are probably someone already involved in a lot of activities. No one interested in sitting around reads a book about living justly.

Maybe you are involved in your church. Maybe you drive three kids to six different lessons or sports events. Maybe you support your spouse in his or her work, and that leaves you with a huge amount of responsibility for cooking and cleaning.

We have seen this firsthand. For nearly four years we ministered in a church plant in the suburbs. I (Will) taught at the church, and Lisa led worship. We know how busy suburban people tend to be. Getting people involved in ministry was like pulling teeth.

In our church we had parents whose kids were in sports every season of every year, several times a week, including Sundays. We had parents whose kids were taking all kinds of lessons—music, dance, art. Parents were struggling to help their children finish the massive amounts of homework piled on them in school these days.

Even if you don't have kids, chances are you are busy as well. This is the nature of the American economy—to keep people busy and buying more stuff. So we work long hours to buy bigger houses or a bigger car. Even when we do find time away from work to enjoy recreational activities, we often compete with our neighbors over who played the best golf course, who has the bigger boat, or who took the more exotic vacation. We are trapped by, yet strangely attracted to, the American suburban experience.

Lisa and I are also busy. We have three kids between the ages of ten and seventeen. One is in public school, one is in private school, and one is homeschooled. Lisa is a full-time writer, and I am a full-time student. We manage a house, maintain family relationships, have friendships that require tending, and work in ministry. If you want to talk busy, we would love to swap stories.

Whenever we talk to folks about living justly, the first questions people ask relate to the time that will be required. So, before we move any farther, we want you to hear this: we know how busy your schedule can be. We feel your pain. The last thing in the world we want to do is take you away from those things that are important to you. But let's talk about what we are all busy doing.

What Is Culture?

One way we can begin to think about our choices, particularly in relation to how much time we can devote to living justly, is by thinking about the kind of culture we are creating.

Culture is such an interesting word. It comes from the Latin and refers to the notion of cultivating land for the purpose of bringing forth plants. So it is not a stretch to think of culture as those things that spring up from the decisions we make. Culture is simply that which tends to grow in the soil of our choices. But that is not how the church in America has been known to use the word.

One thing you can count on like clockwork is a discussion of "culture wars." Every year as Christmas approaches, a certain segment of both the church and the media begin talking about "the war on Christmas." Stories are written about lawsuits seeking to remove manger scenes from the public square, as are columns about not being able to say "Merry Christmas" in community settings and about schools where kids are unable to celebrate their faith openly.

The culture wars at Christmas are the most predictable. However, at other times throughout the year, we witness heated debates on other topics. Take, for example, the media items about not being able to place monuments to the Ten Commandments in courthouses, or features about school boards forbidding students from praying aloud in school, particularly around the time of graduation. And who could forget the parent who sued to have the phrase "under God" removed from the Pledge of Allegiance?

Christian students from public universities also tell stories of challenges to their beliefs. In these schools a culture of deep suspicion about religion prevails, particularly regarding the Christian faith. Ask any Christian student who has been to one of these schools, and they can usually relate a shocking tale of a professor who mocked or belittled their beliefs, either to their face or in what they taught.

These are familiar tales. While not exactly persecution, such events are nonetheless significant cultural indicators. They are quite real; there is a deep antagonism to expressions of faith in so many places in America.

But Lisa and I wonder if the term *culture war* tends to give a false impression regarding the very definition of culture. For example, in our backyard garden, we grow vegetables and herbs. Not surprisingly, the things that grow spring from what we plant. They do not happen by accident. We have never grown broccoli from a basil plant. We have never seen a carrot miraculously morph into asparagus.

We have come to think this way about the culture in which we live as well. It is an organic thing. Sometimes what springs up is quite intentional, such as those things we plant. Other organic cultures are somewhat less intentional.

Consider a lawn. Things grow there whether we want them to or not. We do not need to care for our lawn, mow it, or even water it for this to happen. It seems that no matter how well or how poorly we care for our lawn, something grows there.

But when we do not tend to the lawn, we lose control over what happens there. The grass gets long and attracts bugs. Weeds and poison ivy spring up in the most inconvenient places. This happens simply as a result of the culture of a lawn.

There are places in this country where grass does not grow—in fact, nothing grows. We have friends who moved into a depressed area of Camden, New Jersey. Near their house are brownfields. These federally designated areas are so polluted, nothing will grow in them for decades or centuries. No tending has been given in these fields for some time, and any attention given them was to misuse them, often for short-term gain.

Perhaps these different examples are more like the way we should be thinking about the culture in which we live. There are fertile places that grow good things, which are intentional and consistent with the culture created. There are also the places where things grow whether we want them to or not. And sadly, because of lack of planning, nurture, and proper cultivation, and even because of adverse measures taken to destroy them, there are places where things cannot grow for some time without some significant rehabilitation of the soil.

These three types of fields have much to teach us as we seek to understand culture as the things that grow in the soil we cultivate. And maybe that is the best way to think about what happens if you do not answer the call to live justly. Perhaps this is why Jesus told so many stories about fields and vineyards and creating fertile areas.

Jesus understood something about human nature and the way we live. Humans have a tendency to let things pass and hope they will get better on their own. Perhaps the reason so many farming illustrations are utilized in the Bible is because they help us understand what happens when we don't think carefully about our choices. They help us think properly about our culture. When we ignore the issues surrounding our choices and the kind of culture created by them, weeds tend to spring up—weeds of indifference, and sometimes antagonism, toward the Christian faith.

We can ignore the problems of the ecosystem long enough and abuse that system to the point where a brownfield is the result—just like the antagonism toward the Christian faith that exists in so many places of our country. Perhaps those results tend to grow in a field that has been misused, dumped on, and abused for too long.

The best choice among these is for us all to tend the soil. We can purposely plant good things. We can pull the weeds and give our plants much care. In this type of field, the work of the kingdom is flourishing and growing, producing good fruit.

What Happens If I Don't Answer?

So, back to the original question: "Can't I just answer 'too busy'?" Sure, as long as you realize "too busy" is an answer with deep consequences. In this culture, when you ignore questions of justice, weeds, poison plants, and eventually brownfields spring up. This is what we believe happened in relation to the culture wars in this country. The church has failed in large ways to tend the cultural soil we have been given charge over, and unhealthy "plants" have grown there. You can blame the thorns, or you can ask why the thorns were able to grow in the first place. We suggest the second method.

None of us are passively engaged in God's field. Even those who are not followers of Jesus impact the world system every day in big and small ways. So, do you have to answer God's call to live justly? Certainly not. But realize that something happens when you do not answer. This is not a neutral call. All people, including those who are part of the American church, interact with and are shaped by culture all the time. We do not stand apart from culture. We cannot.

This is where the metaphor gets messy for people of faith. We are called to be cultivators and, in some unusual way, also part of the plants being grown. These are not simply short-term issues. The decisions we make today have culture-shaping ramifications for both the kind of life we are leading now and the kind of world our children will inherit.

Inaction is not the same as acting wrongly. This whole concept of justice should not feel like some massive guilt trip. You can choose to sit it out. The people you connect with can make the same choice, and so can those who connect with them. But while each person individually may have little negative impact on whether this world is just, together the effect is enormous.

Let's think about this issue in economic terms. Though Americans tend to think of economics as dealing with money, it is actually the theory of choice. It is a discipline that studies the total effects of the decisions each person makes. Questions of justice should be seen through this lens. Each of us, by acting in particular ways, creates a system that is more or less just.

Suddenly you may feel the whole idea of justice is a little scary. Even if you answer this call, maybe your neighbor won't, and then his Uncle Frank won't, and egad! This is all too much.

Relax. Let's start small. Let's break this down and see where we can begin. Thinking systemically about the decisions we make is the first step toward thinking and living in keeping with God's heartbeat of justice. Begin viewing yourself as connected into the world in deep and complex, yet very real, ways.

Answering the Call of Justice

We have used metaphors for growing things throughout this chapter, so maybe the best place to begin is by thinking about the food you eat. Every night in our house, as we pray for our food, we try to thank God for all the people that helped get the food to our table. Sometimes that's easy to imagine, such as when we get beets directly from our local, community farmer.

Usually it is more difficult to imagine how food got to us. How exactly does shredded cheese get into a bag? Who picked those strawberries from California? Who placed them in the plastic basket? Who covered them with plastic wrap, arranged them in boxes, loaded and unloaded them from the truck, and arranged them on the store shelf? And when you add up each individual food item used in a meal, the number of hands God uses to bring us our meals is considerable.

Food also touches on so many possible questions of justice. For example, how was the food grown? If you eat fast food or much of the off-the-shelf food available in your grocery store, there is a good chance that what you are eating contains a large amount of corn-based products.

America produces many tons of corn because government policies promote such action. We have such a massive overproduction of corn that we can sell these corn-derived products to food producers, who put them in everything from chicken nuggets to soda. Oddly enough, however, in order to produce so much corn, farmers require massive amounts of petroleum-based fertilizers. At the time of this writing, the price of gasoline in America is at an all-time high, which is based, at least in part, on global unrest and war. So in some weird but fairly direct way, that Twinkie in aisle 12 is linked to all the struggles around obtaining oil in the Middle East.

Yikes. Let's take it down a notch and think about the people involved in the food chain. Migrant workers pick much of the food not harvested by big machines, food like lettuce and tomatoes. While no hard statistics are available, it is estimated that immigrant workers pick between 50 and 80 percent of our fruits and vegetables. So the current immigration debate in America is directly related to what you will serve for dinner tonight.

How about the grocery store employees? What are they paid? Is it fair? Are they carrying a heavy financial burden, perhaps living without insurance or medical care, so that you can pay ten cents less for a dozen eggs? Do you shop for groceries based solely on price, or do you consider the implications of a world where the store with the lowest price wins?

Okay, even that may be too heavy a place to start. Let's just think about the food we eat and how we live based on that food. Twenty-five percent of Americans are significantly overweight.[9] Organizations like the World Health Organization call this condition *overnutrition*, or taking in far more calories than necessary or healthy. Not surprisingly, America leads the world in this condition, with the church heading the charge. According to one recent study, there is a significant relationship between being Christian in America and being overweight.[10] The end result of this condition is poor physical health and correspondingly poor psychological health. We are, quite simply, consuming ourselves to death. Seen this way, we realize the direct connection between food, spirituality, and health.

This is a theme that comes up in Scripture a number of times. Ironically, as we spoke about earlier, we often read certain passages of Scripture with a bias toward the issues we care about. Consider, for example, Ezekiel 16:44–59, a passage that deals with the destruction of Sodom. Rather than being a direct statement about homosexuality, for which the metaphor of Sodom is often applied, this passage instead deals with food: "This was the guilt of your sister Sodom: she and her daughters had pride, excess of food, and prosperous ease, but did not aid the poor and needy" (v. 49).

You have no doubt heard homosexuality condemned as a sin from the pulpit. How often have we heard a sermon about the sin of not sharing what we have with those in need?

MEDITATION BY JANA RIESS

Chaucer once wrote that great peace is found in little busyness. I think of this sometimes when I am staring at a lengthy, quotidian to-do list, full of tasks both work-related and domestic that I need to accomplish in a given day. Often, the peace eludes me. Amidst the post office errand and the grocery trip and the pile of emails I am supposed to slog through, where is that great peace?

Americans have apotheosized busyness so wholly that any peace that daily tasks might once have afforded us has been squeezed out in a mad dash for the finish line. I have to wonder to what extent we have substituted busyness for effectiveness, especially on a relational level. Because, of course, it is in relationship that the seeds of justice are planted and sown. As Will and Lisa point out, choosing not to tend a garden is in itself a choice. When we are so busy that we become what a friend of mine calls "busy-rable" (rhymes with "miserable")—unable to reach out to others because we are so consumed with our own tasks and schedules and desires—we make the conscious choice not to cultivate the garden of peace and justice. Learning to say no to some tasks has been revolutionary for me, both as a Christian and as a woman. I no longer want to make nice. I want to do good.

Slowly, this decision has led to transformation: every day, at least one of those tasks on my list has the potential to lead to an act of justice. Maybe the woman in front of me at Kroger is trying to make a way out of no way with her food stamps. Perhaps when I'm walking to the dry cleaner, I'll have a chat with my widowed neighbor who seems to have nobody left in the world. Whatever it will be today, I want to be free enough from "busy-rableness" that I am open to giving and receiving justice. And it's amazing how, with this perspective, it seems that Chaucer was right: I feel at peace, knowing that the mundane can and will lead to the extraordinary.

7   OPPOSITION FROM THE INSIDE

Every once in a while a moment of grace envelops people completely, and Christine knew she was in the middle of one. The warmth of Jenna and Randy felt like a salve she didn't realize she needed so badly. It started the moment they got out of the car, ready to hear why they were such terrible people. Christine wondered when the other shoe would drop.

Jenna was waiting at the front door, dressed in bright blue Capris and a T-shirt that said "Plate's Full" in bold letters, a very relaxed ensemble for her. "Come on in, you guys! We're so glad you came!"

Randy hollered from the kitchen. "Come on back, Matt! I'm marinating the steaks right now."

Jenna leaned down and hugged Toby, ending a kiss on the softness of his neck with a raspberry. "You kids go on into the backyard. The trampoline's set up."

Laurel, Zach, and Toby sped through the house to the back doors.

"Watch out for your little brother!" Christine called after them.

Jenna tucked her arm through Christine's. "Come on back. I'm making my homemade coleslaw." The hit of church suppers. Christine could eat nothing but that and be as happy as

Antoine with a Little Debbie. "I'd offer to help, but I wouldn't want to ruin perfection."

"You can foil up the baked potatoes."

They set to work at the kitchen island, chatting about the kids, Christine wondering what this was really all about. She kept waiting.

Finally, after they'd eaten their meal, concocted s'mores in front of the fire pit outside, and settled the kids, sugarcoated inside and out, in the family room to watch a movie, Randy invited them to sit on the deck. Jenna brought out a pot of coffee and some mugs.

This is it.

Christine hadn't had such a relaxing time in months, and she told them so.

"Well, you all have been busy, and we wanted to give you some downtime." Randy handed a mug to Matt.

"That's right," Jenna chimed in.

Matt shook his head. "Guys, I really thought you would be upset with us for pulling out of most of our church responsibilities."

Jenna nodded. "We were, Matt. I was mad as a hornet, if you want to know the truth."

"Boy, was she," Randy agreed.

Christine wasn't surprised. "What happened?"

Jenna swatted at a mosquito on her arm. "I was sitting at a leadership meeting mouthing off—sorry, but it's true and I apologize—and I saw myself actually criticizing you for building houses, feeding homeless people, and spending time with at-risk teenagers. My gosh! And a couple of others were happy to jump on my bandwagon, and when I saw what I was leading the charge against, I realized I was doing the work of Satan."

"That's a little strong, isn't it?" Matt said.

"Is it?" She leaned over and took her mug off the table, cradling it with both hands and holding it close against her chest. "So I came home to Randy and told him that if we're the only ones who support you in what you're doing, so be it."

Christine could hardly believe what she was hearing. "I can't begin to tell you how relieved I am!" She started to laugh, getting to her feet to give Jenna and Randy a hug.

She called Yvette the next day and told her all about it.

"Honey, hold those folks close to your heart, because they are the sugar in your coffee. I have a feeling, with the way you and Matt are sold out, you'll be going further up and deeper in, and people like Randy and Jenna will help see you through."

"I feel like what they're doing is a ministry in and of itself."

"Oh, it is, baby. They're using the gift of encouragement. And that's something we just don't have enough of these days. You know, God's not going to call everybody to the mission, but I feel safe in saying he's calling all of us to be an encouragement to those who lend a hand. Just a kind word means the world, doesn't it?"

Yvette told her that Antoine had come running in looking for Christine the other day after he fell off his scooter again. "Christine, the boy thinks you're his personal nurse or something. Oh, he'll let us bind his wounds, but he doesn't like it!"

Later, Christine stopped by her mother's on the way home from lunch duty at school. Ever since her parents' divorce, Christine felt like she was a surrogate spouse, and it was getting worse.

Her mother invited her back to the kitchen for a cup of coffee. "I don't know when the last time we had a cup of coffee was."

"Last week?"

"Was it? It seems so much longer than that."

She called Matt on her cell phone as she backed out of the driveway. "Am I wrong that this bugs me?"

"She's manipulating you. Or trying to. You've got every right to feel annoyed, babe."

"I feel like I'm not being who she needs me to be. I feel like I'm disappointing her at every turn." She turned onto the main drag, heading toward the bank.

"Well, babe, I don't think that can be helped."

"But I feel so bad."

"Have you thought about having a serious discussion with her about all this?"

"She'll freak, Matty."

"Probably. Have you talked to your dad about it yet?"

"No. I can't get a word in edgewise since he started dating that woman."

She just didn't see that coming. Her father dating again? It made her feel a little creepy-crawly, to tell the truth.

"You're going to have to talk to your mom."

"But I don't want to." She felt her lip jut out.

"Want me to go with you?"

"No!"

"Okay, just thought I'd offer."

"I think I understand that verse where Jesus said to hate your mother and father, brother and sister, so you could follow him. Not that I really hate her. I just can't do what she wants me to do."

"It's a toughie."

She pulled up to the drive-through window at the bank. "I gotta go."

❒

Christine slipped into the seat next to Antoine's grandmother, Stella. "Sorry I'm late," she whispered. "Traffic was a nightmare!"

"He hasn't sung yet. You're just in time."

This was the first time Antoine had asked anything more of her than some hugs and Band-Aids. He had a solo in the school talent show. The same excitement she felt at Laurel's concerts jangled her insides.

He walked out into the spotlight, so small and yet so large. The child had a presence about him. She couldn't wait to see what he would be when he grew up. He nodded to the piano player, and Christine giggled. "He knows what to do, doesn't he?"

"He sure does."

When the strains of *The Old Rugged Cross* issued from him clean and pure, sending warm ice down Christine's spine, she pressed her hand to her mouth to keep the tears at bay.

"You go on and cry." Stella handed her a tissue. "That child's got the gift."

Afterward, just like she did with her own children, Christine took Antoine out for ice cream. They had to drive a ways, but Stella, only about five years older than Christine, chatted about her job at the airport and her poor daughter, Antoine's mother, who had disappeared a few years before. Stella said the Lord had told her that her daughter was still alive and fine, and she always believed what the Spirit said. "Do you believe what the Spirit says, Christine?"

"I try to, Stella. But sometimes it's hard."

"Following the Lord is usually hard. But I guess, with what I've seen in my life, it's the only thing that makes any sense."

◻

Okay, Matt could play tough too. Miss Smarty Pants at home searching the Internet for injustice—well, he could do the same. He called her. "I'm challenging you to a duel."

"Ooh, sexy."

He looked out of his office door to see if anyone heard. Of course not, but he couldn't help himself.

"Okay, so you're doing this 'further up and deeper in' stuff Yvette talked about, which is fine. Although all the stuff at home seems a little over the top."

She'd been harping on the AC lately too. Seventy-six degrees, and he was a sweaty kind of guy. Sometimes he thought she was being too intentional. But she was so good at it, he had to admit.

"You sound testy."

"I am a little cranky. It's the right thing to do, but I'm a little cranky. So anyway, I thought, 'Why let Chris have all the fun?'"

"And?"

"And we're taking a bus trip down to West Virginia in a couple of weeks to witness firsthand what the coal mining industry is doing to people."

"Really?" Silence. "Do you have a fever?"

"I wish. I'm thinking maybe it'll make me not so mad that you're going around turning lights off all the time when we can afford it."

"I'm game. Can we take the kids?"

"Yep. It would be good for them to see, I think. By the way, it's called mountaintop removal mining."

"I'm already logging on."

"THAT'S NOT HOW WE DO IT AROUND HERE"

Kiss normal good-bye.

This is the best advice we can give you. All of us exist in a series of relationships that are bound together by common interests and common life decisions. We all come from families that trained us to think in certain ways. We join churches or synagogues or other faith communities that worship or think about questions of God the way we do. We participate in organizations that seek to accomplish the things we currently care about. We vote for candidates we believe hold to our common interests and will shape the culture to move in the direction of our shared desires for the world.

If you start asking questions about those common interests and desires, as well as the structures that flow from those commonalities, you can expect opposition, frustration, and counterquestions from those who are often the closest to you. These are people with whom you share a wealth of experiences. This will be particularly true if you begin to realize that the systems in which you have participated are not neutral and deeply affect whether the world is more just.

What is considered normal was redefined the morning of September 11, 2001. I (Will) remember it like it was yesterday. I was in my office, two blocks from the White

House, in downtown DC. I was waiting for a phone call from a vendor in Manhattan. Someone came running through the halls, calling us to crowd around a portable TV as we watched the towers collapse. Minutes later we were on the roof of our building. We could not see the Pentagon directly, but the smoke was unavoidable, billowing up and blackening the sky.

The city was filled with pandemonium. I got as far as Union Station, the main terminal for all commuter trains in and out of DC, and I was stopped. No one knew what was going to happen. It took me nearly six hours and four modes of transportation to get home that day. We knew things had changed.

For a few months afterward, I walked past armed guards every day on my way to the office. It seemed we would never get back to normal—whatever that had been before that fateful day. In many ways we have not. At the time of this writing, American troops are in Iraq, fighting a mission that is now justified as having to do with the terror of 9/11. Regularly we hear news stories about foiled terrorist plots, and recently threats have caused people to be unable to carry toothpaste and shampoo on board airplanes.

Yet in a very real way, things have gone on since 9/11. The stock market reopened. People started flying again. New terrors and fears—international, domestic, and even personal—came to crowd out the vision of the towers crashing or the Pentagon burning. After that fateful day, "normal" was redefined for the whole world.

When we say "kiss normal good-bye," we are not referring to some major cataclysmic event that will change everything you know. The kind of normal we are talking about in this regard is entrenched far deeper into our lives. It is the normal of the everyday, where changes happen more slowly.

Our relationships—including our families, our neighbors, friends from work, the places we worship, and the civic organizations in which we participate—are all the result of the decisions we have made. Now, imagine you start to question some of those decisions. The simple fact is that being involved in a life of justice will have deep effects on every relationship you currently enjoy.

For example, consider again how we eat. A number of years ago I (Will) began asking questions about what I was eating. I cut out processed sugar, I reduced my caffeine intake, and I started reading the labels on food I purchased. I engaged in a long-term project to eat well. After sugar and caffeine—they were the easy targets—I began to look at the actual processing of foods. I learned about the way animals are often raised for meat in America, with tons of hormones and other unhealthy additives.

I changed my diet, needless to say. This was easy to do for myself. It was much harder to accomplish for the whole family. As in many suburban families, our kids had grown up eating the food that comes from the shelves of the standard grocery store. I began to understand that eating this way was causing a whole series of problems for our children. In the short term, I began to realize that the food they were eating was causing attention issues that affected them academically. Over their life, if we did not change the way they ate, we would open them up to disease and significant health problems. So slowly I set out to change the way we as a household ate. The whole family grumbled.

Chicken nuggets were replaced with grilled fish. Macaroni and cheese was replaced with rice. Sugary and salty snacks were replaced with nuts and fruit. Over time the kids came to accept this way of eating. While we still delve into the realm of unhealthy eating from time to time (I confess I have a pack of Cheddarwursts in the fridge even now), our children expect to look in the pantry and find healthy food to eat or to come to the dinner table and get a healthy meal.

But this decision was not without consequence. Meals together are sacred. After all, they were the metaphor Christ used to speak of our eucharistic bond. A complete change in what and how much we ate forced a redefinition of meals together. There is a reason they call certain types of food "comfort food," and it was far more comfortable to eat the old way. This change we began to enact was tricky enough to navigate within our own family. Imagine going to church suppers!

We think this helps illustrate what happens when you begin asking questions about living justly. It will have an impact on even the seemingly mundane aspects of life.

A great story from the life of Jesus speaks to this issue. He had been going throughout the country healing people, restoring sight, and giving life back to the diseased and physically infirm. In Matthew 12, his mother and his brothers came to him and, in the nicest possible way, told him, "Dude, we think you're nuts."

Okay, so the Bible does not use those exact words. But from the passage, his family and friends clearly thought he was not making the right decisions, and they decided to call him back to his senses. This was from the woman who had been part of the events surrounding his miraculous birth and early childhood, including personal angelic visitations, dream messages, hosts of angels, and surprise royal visitors. Jesus's family delivered their message to the man who would be the Savior of the world, the one not only preaching the kingdom of God on earth but also backing it up with some pretty amazing acts.

If Jesus did not escape scrutiny, you won't either. You are bound together with those around you. We talked earlier about religion, meaning those values that bind us together. This applies to the whole of our lives. Our lives are simply the web of relationships formed by a common view of the world. If you start challenging that view, be prepared—your life and many of your relationships will never be the same again.

Maintaining Love

Before we go any further, permit us to stop and make one really important point: relationships are all you have. You have a family of some kind. So we cannot emphasize enough the importance of doing all that you can in love.

This is where the teachings of Jesus are hard to navigate. When his family and friends came to question his sanity, he responded by saying, "Who is my mother, and who are my brothers?" (Matt. 12:48). Is this how you are to respond? Well, yes and no.

The kingdom of God requires primacy. It comes first. We believe this is what Jesus was getting at with his seemingly harsh words. When people convert to the ways of Jesus, or any faith tradition, they make some kind of statement of commitment. This pledge obliges them to see the world differently. Converting to faith means they agree to living with a new code, a new standard for values and decisions and relationships. But at the same time, what they commit to is a relationship.

We fear that too much of the contemporary church sees conversion to Christianity as simply an intellectual decision. It is that, partly. In the book of Proverbs, Solomon exhorts the listener this way: "My child, do not forget my teaching" (Prov. 3:1). The way of God has always possessed an element of intellectual assent. But consider what follows on the heels of this call: "Do not let loyalty and faithfulness forsake you; bind them around your neck, write them on the tablet of your heart. So you will find favor and good repute in the sight of God and of people" (vv. 3–4).

The primary activity of God has been to shape a particular people who follow this God in particular ways. This is important to remember when you start to ask questions about living justly in the world. Jesus seemed to understand this implicitly. The disciples had fears about their new life and what it would cost them. They even questioned the very identity of Jesus. In answer to these concerns, Jesus said, "I am the way, and the truth, and the life" (John 14:6). We have always found it interesting that Jesus claimed to be "the way," which speaks of a relationship and a culture, before he claimed to be "the truth."

Each of us is accountable for living out the call of God in our lives. Each of us is responsible to shape families and other cultural systems that speak to what Doug Pagitt calls God's "hopes, dreams, and aspirations for this world."[11] It is a world whose creation we are participating in, and the best way to show the power of God's work in our lives is to participate and invest in loving relationships. Jesus said this himself: "By this everyone will know that you are my disciples, if you have love for one another" (John 13:35).

This hardly matches our contemporary cultural desires. As products of Western society, we like to have things settled. We like to know the right answer. It is much easier to feel that we have our lives together when we're responsible only for ourselves. By inviting you to join us on a life of justice, we invite you to a life of ambiguity on a road traveled by others who are equally unsure of where they are heading. We invite you to join with those who seek to become radical followers of God. And these followers are a group with a long and checkered history.

The church has always struggled to know how to live rightly in this world. The greatest evidence of this is the consistent five-hundred-year reinvention in which the church has regularly engaged. After Jesus departed this earth, things were pretty exciting for the early church. However, for a period of time, between about AD 325 and AD 476, the church rethought everything about the way she lived in the world.

In AD 1052, the church went through another reinvention with a massive split between the eastern and western church over issues of doctrine. (And you thought church splits were a contemporary phenomenon and only happened over the color of the carpet.) The 1500s saw another major shift in the church with the Protestant Reformation, which divided the church yet again.

Now, here we sit in the early 2000s, and we should be conscious of the fact that the people of God have always struggled with what it means to live faithfully as one body. When we sense a need to live differently because of the call of God on our lives, some proper humility is in order. Like the reformed smoker who wants to tell anyone and everyone who will listen about her newfound knowledge, you will be tempted to call everyone to join you. And we think you should—in love. Keep your relationships. Maintain your bonds. Live justly, but do so in a way that is winsome and calls others to join in.

We are called to live differently while maintaining relationships. This is the paradox of becoming radical followers of Jesus in a life of justice. We will face opposition. Things that were once easy will not be easy anymore.

Recently we were at a gathering of folks we've known for a long time. Our views differ on a lot of things now, one of them being our commitment to peace. But we decided that to engage in conversations that are anything but peaceful would be testifying against what we believe. Certainly there is a time to speak up, to offer opinions, hopes, and dreams, but we must exercise caution and love.

In Colossians 1:28, Paul talks about his desire to present everyone "mature in Christ." Maturity is to be the goal of all people of faith. The word *maturity* carries with it the idea of some future goal, but when you look at the way the word was used in Paul's time, it also speaks of the actual process to maturity. So we invite you to a process that will be long and confusing and may involve some difficult choices. You are being called to the difficult task of living differently while winsomely calling all around to join in the race.

MEDITATION BY DOUG PAGITT

Sixteen years ago, my wife, Shelley, and I decided we would make a videotape blessing for Michon, our daughter, at each birthday. The idea was to give her a living diary of our hopes and desires for her. In 1991 it was easy to set up the video camera, drop in the VHS tape, point it at the couch, hit record, and leave a blessing. Somehow that was the only year we pulled it off.

Recently, at the beginning of her sixteenth year, I watched the video. It terrified me. The video was meant to help Michon trace her family faith legacy; what it has done instead is show me the deep change that has taken place within me.

I not only looked different and a lot younger, I also sounded different. What I said in 1991 I have a hard time agreeing with now. So much has changed. Many of the things that were important to me back then are no longer important a decade and a half later. And things that are so important to me now were not even on my mind back then.

Viewing this tape and recognizing how much I have changed prompts me to consider what kind of faith I have raised my daughter in—a changing one, for sure.

I would like to believe that I have raised my daughter "in the way she ought to go," but "the way" has evolved. When I made that tape, I wanted her not to forget my teaching, but now I hope she will do just that. I want her to disregard much of what I told her.

I wonder, *What kind of parent was I?* I worry that raising a child in an atmosphere of volatile theological and spiritual change was not good for her. I worry that she needed consistency. But at this point, that is not an option. Her faith has been shaped by a dynamism of progression, for better or worse.

123

And maybe for the better. Maybe a model of evolving faith is just what is needed to live in a world of great change. Maybe Michon has learned from our changing practice of faith not to lock into just one way of thinking and living. Maybe she will know deeply in her being that she ought to go easy on people with whom she disagrees because, just like her dad, they may be perfectly confident in things now that they will question later.

Maybe Michon was raised "in the way she ought to go" after all—one filled with rebirth and resurrection. Maybe she is truly prepared to follow the God of re-creation and to join with God in the blessing of all the world.

P.S. I wonder what I will think of what I've written when I'm celebrating my granddaughter's sixteenth birthday. Maybe it will still make sense to me then. Maybe. I hope so.

8 | "ARE YOU NEW AROUND HERE?"

*O**kay, I am in an alternate universe**, Christine thought
as she boarded the bus. Politically she always thought
of herself as her own girl, voting her conscience and
not the party line, but environmental issues never really sat
first and foremost on her agenda. In fact, environmentalists
sort of bugged her with their self-righteousness; the fact that
they sometimes resorted to violence horrified her as much as
abortion clinic bombings. But now, sitting among a group of
people clearly not of her tribe, well, she felt like a poseur, to
use the Laurel and Britney vernacular.

What a bunch. Most of them were dressed in outdoorsy
clothing, some had extra piercings, some sprouted dread-
locks—and that wouldn't have been so bad if they weren't
eyeing her with such suspicion that it practically oozed from
their Chaco sandals and their hemp clothing.

*I knew I shouldn't have worn this skort. And pink? What
was I thinking?*

Well, she wasn't thinking. Comfortable in her own world, she never really dreamed of something else, and this was truly something else. They could at least smile at her kids. Would that be so hard? But no matter. She was traveling down to West Virginia to see the devastation, not party with these folks.

And man! Why did I have to bring chicken sandwiches for lunch? They were probably all vegan members of PETA!

Leather shoes. She was wearing leather shoes. She looked down the aisle. Some Birkenstocks dotted the rubbery walkway. The suede kind. *Oh, good.*

One guy sat down in the bus seat in front of her and Matt. He looked to be in his later years of college, a shrub of curly hair framing his pale face and two buttons pinned to his worn denim jacket. One said, "Jesus Is My President," the other, "Who Would Jesus Bomb?"

"Hey, guys, I'm Rob. You been on one of these things before?"

"No," Matt said. "First time."

"Me too," Christine chimed in.

"Thought so."

Just great.

"Well, stick with me. I can get you into places around that mine so you can see things way up close."

Christine leaned forward. "Why is everybody so quiet?" she whispered.

Rob leaned close to her face and whispered just as low, "Because everybody's too serious." Then he laughed. "Don't worry. They'll lighten up. You know you all look pretty strange in those country-club clothes."

"I know."

"It's kinda like coming to the clown convention in a wet suit or something, you know? But no sweat. I'm glad you're here. What a lot of these guys don't know is that if the soccer moms and dads don't get on board, we're sunk."

Soccer mom? She liked this kid.

◻

The woman standing beside Christine tied her windbreaker around her waist. "My goodness, it's already warm today, isn't it?"

"I know. So much for the weather reports. Feels like August instead of June." Christine reached into her green backpack— not a forest green, not an earthy green, but that bright lime green. "I've got some water. Would you like a bottle?"

"Thank you, I would. I'm Martha, by the way."

"Christine, and nice to meet you." Christine pulled out the bottle and handed it over, noting the woman's hand. A simple wedding band encircled the ring finger on her left hand, and she wore a bracelet watch, inexpensive and with the look of the Wal-Mart jewelry counter. The pale peach fingernail polish reflected a pearlish sunlight. Arthritis inflated several knuckles.

Christine felt a little shell-shocked. Earlier they'd gathered in a cinderblock community church in a hamlet, whose main street was lined only with houses, a now-defunct storefront it appeared somebody decided to make a home, and this place to worship. She'd never seen a sadder collection of buildings in her life. Pastor Mumfrey, who double-dutied as a coal miner and had lived there all fifty-three years of his life, spoke about what life was like down in this hollow when he was a boy. "Streams I used to go catchin' crawdaddies in are like different places. I have to move aside the sediment just to see the rocks." The wide smile almost never left his face, though, and Christine wondered which house he lived in. The most luxurious one was a simple, well-kept rancher, three bedrooms at the most. The most substandard made her want to cry, especially for the little blond boy as skinny as a cricket, who was sitting on the railing of the porch, dangling stringy legs weighed down with dirty feet.

Laurel didn't escape the feeling either. Keeping close to her mother, her eyes looked as big as the plates the church

127

members had brought for the potluck they'd thrown for the group's lunch. "Oh, Mom," she said over and over again.

But Christine had to laugh inside at how uncomfortable some of those young activists seemed in that building where she felt at home. When Pastor Mumfrey blessed the food, she suddenly realized she wasn't just fighting for folks without much of a voice, she was actually rolling up her sleeves for a brother. This portion of the body had been stripped by poverty and exploited by the Goliaths of the coal industry. Where were the other Christians? Then again, that might not be fair. Just because she was the only Christian of her ilk didn't mean that others never lifted a finger.

Still, she couldn't remember any of those religious radio personalities talking about stuff like this. Coal companies made money, and while she heard a lot of stepping on toes on the radio and was thankful for it, it seemed like big business had become some sort of sacred cow.

Then again, she'd only just become aware of this herself. It was so easy to slip into self-righteousness. Too easy.

Shame on me, she had thought.

Now, as the group moved toward the place where a mountain was being dismantled, Christine held Toby's hand, and Matt slipped Zach into the child backpack he always strapped on his back. Laurel had just remembered she was still a little miffed at missing a birthday party. They walked with Martha up a gravel road with rusted corpses of automobiles left alongside.

Flyrock. She still couldn't get over the thought.

Pastor Mumfrey had talked about flyrock, the pieces of mountain that hurtled through the air after a blast and sometimes crashed through house windows, landed on cars, or split roofs, occasionally causing injury or even death. She couldn't believe there was a slangy buzzword for this. She said so to Martha.

Martha trudged upward. "You know, you work all your life to make a home, take care of it, raise a family in its walls, and it can be destroyed and nobody cares. Not the coal companies, not the government, nobody."

"It's terrible."

Rob loped up alongside her. "Take this path right here."

She followed him, agreeing with Matt he'd better keep the kids with the rest of the group.

Rob held aside the boughs of trees that sometimes grew over the pathway, and after climbing higher up the forested mountain, they approached the edge of the path. The site spread before them—roads and machinery, a network of pits and holes that gutted the earth. When seeing it from this vantage point, she was reminded of termites, vermin that destroyed a place someone had built with their own hands, a place in which to live and grow and love. Only this someone was God, and his very creation was raping the place he had created for his creatures, his plants, his people, to thrive.

"Oh, Lord," she whispered.

Rob shoved his hands in his pockets. "The pictures just don't replace the real thing, do they?"

"Not even close."

"That mountain used to be higher than the one we're standing on. And now it's gone."

Normally Bible verses didn't spring to Christine's head, but she said out loud, "The earth is the Lord's, and the fulness thereof; the world, and they that dwell therein."

The reflection of the ravaged scenery mirrored in the sadness on his face, Rob continued, "For he hath founded it upon the seas, and established it upon the floods."

Christine couldn't wrench her eyes from the devastation as she watched trucks haul the coal off the site, trucks she'd heard earlier plowed these roads at too high a speed, carving deep potholes and forcing citizens off the road, sometimes to their destruction.

One lady had testified at the church about the death of her twenty-one-year-old daughter, who had been run off a narrow mountain lane by a coal truck. "They get paid by the load," she said. And she held high her child's senior portrait.

Christine wiped the tears away.

This absolute disregard for God's creation turned the flame up inside her. "You know, I came down here thinking about the people affected. I'm all about people, especially kids, you know?" She licked her lips. "But seeing this, I understand what lousy stewards we've become, destroying the beauty of God's work for our own gain. How did we ever get here?"

"Preach it, Christine."

"All so the coal companies can make a dollar more a ton. That's what gets me."

Later on, they trudged up yet another hill a few miles away, this one, according to the itinerary, a driveway leading to the home of someone trying to get someone else to care that the mountain behind her home was crumbling down and threatening her home. The mountain had once housed a mine, and a blowout had caused a stream to run through her garage. Nobody held themselves accountable, even though funds had been set aside for cases such as hers.

Christine expected to find a house at the end of the drive, maybe one of those little three-bedroom ranchers with a black iron initial tacked to the fireplace and a round garden with a birdbath out front. But no, an older trailer rested on a well-cared-for lawn. The garage stood apart from the home, and a small stream of water ran across the cement and onto the gravel.

Martha got up to speak, to tell her story.

So this was the home she'd worked for all her life.

The flame turned up even higher inside of Christine. How much more could she take? How much weight of knowledge could she bear?

On the bus ride home, she turned around and tried to chat with the man behind her. He spoke with a thick accent—it sounded German to her—wore John Lennon glasses and a black turtleneck, and wanted nothing to do with her. Actually, his face reminded her of Ozzie Osbourne. Funny.

It's okay. These people haven't seen the last of me.

❏

Laurel ran up to Matt as he entered the house through the door to the garage. He'd been hoping to find Christine right away, get the news out before he chickened out.

"Dad, look! A picture of Pascal!"

"Neat, sweetie." He set down his briefcase, took the picture, and eyed the little boy, licorice eyes staring out of a face the color of espresso. Handing the photo back, he said, "Where's Mommy?" He didn't want to share the news from Clifton. In fact, he wondered how long it would take Christine to bounce back this time.

"In the den."

"What's for dinner?"

Laurel shrugged. "Yucky natural food, probably."

Matt patted her between the shoulder blades. "I've got to have a serious talk with Mom."

She inhaled. "Are you guys getting a divorce?"

"Why do you always ask that? We're fine. It's got nothing to do with our marriage, okay, sweetie?" Laurel couldn't take their disagreements. And they'd been disagreeing over the house lately. But right now, none of that mattered.

"Okay. I'll go put a movie on for Zach and Toby."

"Cool, thanks."

He walked down the central hall, past the bathroom, and into the main entryway. Looked like the kids had been out picking flowers. Three water glasses overflowed with blooms, one of them holding only submerged flower heads—Zach's, of course.

The den sat to the left of the front door. The builders called it the library. *Yeah, right*, Matt had thought. *This is a spare room!* Nevertheless, he had always liked to think he had a library, even if it did hold just a couple of bookshelves, the computer desk, and all the junk that Christine had been culling for Helping Hands. She sat at the desk, slung low in the chair, one leg hanging off the chair arm, keyboard in her lap.

"Hey, hon!" she said. "You're home a little early. I was just about to make supper."

"Hey, can we go sit on the deck? I need to tell you something."

"Something's wrong?" She placed the keyboard aside and stood up.

"Yeah."

She shoved her feet into a nearby pair of pink flip-flops and led him down the hallway and out back. "What happened?"

"I got a call from Clifton on my way home." He reached out and encircled her forearm with a gentle grasp. "Babe, Antoine was riding on his scooter today when a driver rounded the corner too fast. He was probably drunk or something. Yvette didn't know for sure."

"Oh no! Is he going to be okay?"

"No." How could he say this? How could he knowingly break her heart? "Antoine died. He was dead before the paramedics even arrived."

"Oh no!" He drew her close. More tears. More tears.

□

Christine huddled in her walk-in closet, hugging herself as she wept. Every time she tried to force down the grief, swallowing her tears, they returned with more force, as if human heartache had no bottom.

And it didn't.

Amy. Antoine.

She never knew she could feel such pain, such grief, such disillusionment, such anger, such sadness. And on and on it came, like a never-ending bread line.

A soft knock vibrated the closet door. "Come on in."

Jenna's head peered around. "Can I come sit with you?"

"Sure."

She entered the dim sanctuary. "I called to see if Zach and Toby wanted to come play tomorrow, and Matt told me what happened."

Christine said, "Yeah." It was all she had.

Jenna took her hand and they sat together, saying nothing. Every so often Christine would say something about Antoine. And Jenna would squeeze her hand.

Maybe her mother was right. Maybe this all cost too much in the end.

SUBURBANITES AT THE GATE

Every region of America possesses its own jokes of "You're not from around here, are you?" This is true whether you live in the South or New England, and certainly if you are from Texas. Have you ever had one of those jokes told about you? Well, be prepared.

We have recently sought to join with those who are already involved in works of justice. The initial response: guarded suspicion. This is well deserved and is a response you should expect as you look for ways to join in God's work in the world.

We are deeply involved in "mountaintop justice." In coal-rich areas such as Kentucky, West Virginia, and Tennessee, many people are living amid the devastation caused by mountaintop removal. This is precisely what it sounds like. Coal companies literally blast mountains to pieces as a cheaper means of getting to the underlying coal. You can imagine what it looks like in the valley below where people are trying to live. Aside from the effects of the blasting, the water tables are ruined, allergens fill the air, and houses are destroyed. Removing a mountaintop contributes to people living in horrible conditions right here in the United States.

Last summer our community hosted a group of student activists who were giving up part of their vacation to learn about mountaintop removal while working to change this horrible practice. Because our community meets in a house and not a building that looks like a church, we are more easily able to support those working on issues of justice who are not connected to the organized church. Many of these wonderful people claim no faith at all, but they feel comfortable crashing at the house on High Street. Further, because our community has been engaged with this issue for some time now, many in our faith group have made some great relationships with these folks.

However, some people still respond to our involvement with guarded suspicion. I (Lisa) experienced this response our first summer in Lexington. One day I was headed to the pool with the kids. Our community had arranged to bring food to the activists, so on my way to the pool, I planned to stop by the house and bring them some watermelon. I walked in wearing a bathing suit, hair up in a clip and wearing a beach wrap, with three children in tow. Oh yeah, and driving a Volvo wagon. A regular twenty-first-century June Cleaver. It doesn't get any more suburban-looking than that.

The look I got was clear: "You're not from around here, are you?"

I felt really strange. A few guys were very nice and showed us the petition, thanking us for the watermelon. The stares from the others were either bland or, from several of the women, downright hostile. I felt naked and judged standing there with a bunch of excited kids, and, well, they didn't even appreciate my watermelon! I could have lost a thumb on that fruit!

Unfortunately, I didn't enter the community center again while they were there. I felt spurned and a little angry. It wasn't the Jesus response.

It is hard for suburbanites to connect with issues of justice. There are few conditions in the burbs that would cause us to ask questions about those in need. In the burbs, there are few, if any, people without a home; few are dying of AIDS; and few will go to bed hungry. As a result, those from the communities in which most American Christians live are rarely ever challenged to ask questions about how we live in relation to those at the margins of society.

If we were honest with ourselves, some of us would admit that the promise of a carefree life was one of the reasons we moved to the suburbs. Others of us have always lived in the suburbs and haven't realized until recently how sheltered our existence has been. Despite the reasons, questions of justice are hard, and commitment to someone in need is even harder. Who wants to deal with that after the typical nine-to-five workday?

Few would even know how to get involved if they did start to ask these questions. The net result is a broad gap between the suburbs and those who have engaged themselves as "the hands and feet of Jesus" to the poor, disadvantaged, or disenfranchised.

You should be aware of this gap when you begin to engage with folks who may have been working on justice issues for some time, and you should be prepared for the hard work of convincing people you are serious about this work. After all, we look like we do not belong, like we come from someplace other than the world of most people working on issues of justice. For those from the suburbs who decide to engage with these issues, one of the hardest challenges is fitting in. Sometimes we feel like country cousins with straw hats, cardboard suitcases, and lace-up shoes, fresh off the hay wagon and plunked down in Times Square. We do not feel comfortable in the skin of a justice worker.

Often those who join with justice are reacting to the very life many have chosen in the suburbs. The two cars, the Ralph Lauren–clothed kids, the 401(k), the big house with room to spare. But the suburban existence can be a lonely place, just like the rest of the world. And all of us seek to belong to something.

In an effort to show solidarity with those who are working to bring about change in the world, often people develop ways of looking, talking, and acting. This is simply another culture, another way of being. Remember how we defined culture in the previous chapter? The activist look is yet another outworking of people's choices and decisions.

Surprisingly, this look is one of the most difficult issues we have had to navigate. When we first started getting involved in issues of living justly, we did not fit in.

I (Will) am a middle-aged white guy. I wear khakis. I have polo shirts with the names of resorts and vacation locations embroidered on them. Not exactly the typical activist uniform. Lisa wears makeup and earrings and avoids outdoorsy clothing as much as she can. She likes sparkly sandals and pedal pushers.

Nothing has changed about the way we dress. We still drive a Volvo. We still go to the pool. But over time we have developed a rich set of relationships with other people seeking to bring God's voice of love for the poor into the world. So what changed? Time and commitment. That was all.

And yeah, we did buy the Chacos. But hey, if the shoe fits . . .

Recently we went camping with a bunch of mostly young activists in the hills of Tennessee. We were loved and accepted as one of them because we *are* one of them. This is how belonging always works. Someone once told us that it takes three years of being in the same group until you even begin to be honest with each other and reveal your true selves. Are you willing to commit long term to join with others in the work of God, whether you feel comfortable or not?

Be Ready to Serve

We live in a commitment-phobic culture. The average worker graduating from college will switch careers two to five times. In our local grocery store, over two hundred different choices of deodorant line the shelves. Gone are the days when the choices of apples included Red Delicious and Golden Delicious. Even our family has fallen prey to the choices: Fuji, Braeburn, Gala, and Pink Lady. Good-bye Granny Smith! And if you are a typical suburban American Christian, you have probably church shopped more than once. All of these forces work together, making us less likely to commit to something for the long haul. Who wants to miss out?

This is a big problem for us.

It is tempting to blame our lack of consistency and commitment on the marketplace or the globalization of ideas, and while those factors play into this syndrome, this phenomenon is not new. The Old Testament is one long story of God calling people to live one way, and then those people living that way—for a time. Some time periods in Scripture were relatively stable, and God's people remembered their call to "seek the welfare of the city" (Jer. 29:7). But the rest of the Hebrew Bible tells of a people who forgot the way they were to live. They made other choices.

God's people always seem to be getting carried off somewhere to help them think differently about their place in the world. In the strange land, they repented, and God returned them to their homeland. This happened over and over again.

Current economic forces seem to heighten the importance of choice. God doesn't seem to carry off nations anymore, but perhaps the intensifying restlessness we all feel is the same factor at work. Churches now mimic the marketplace and make decisions in a one-year time frame. Some bigger churches seek to reinvent themselves every six months. It is tough to live justly with this type of dynamic. With this short-term thinking, one of two things can happen.

The first is that those who are following Jesus tend to view life choices as nothing more than another market decision, one that we can regularly change. We flit through life with varying commitments to varying concerns. Lisa and I love the idea of short-term missions trips. They can be a great way to introduce people to issues of justice and need both here in the United States and around the world. But life is not a short-term trip. We can't just do good for a week at a time and expect it to count for the rest of the year.

We need to recalibrate our thinking to the long term. We often ask, "What kind of world will our grandchildren inherit if we act this way?" We all can agree this is vitally important for the big decisions. However, this question is just as important to ask for the small choices. Where we buy a house has some effect on the future, but where we buy our clothes may have a much greater effect on whether the world is more just and more people are working for justice in one hundred years.

Where we buy our clothes impacts global economies in ways we may not fathom. The inexpensive shirt or dress may be a product of cheap, sometimes slave, labor in foreign markets. This economic model is unsustainable and may be leading toward more difficult economic conditions in the future.

The second effect of short-term thinking is that those who are involved in long-term works grow mistrustful of outsiders. So much of today's activism on issues of justice such as the environment and human rights is being driven by a perceived belief that our institutions, including the church, have neglected to engage in acts of justice. When we show up on the scene, they have every right to be suspicious.

We need to commit to the hard work of joining in. It will not be easy. We love to belong, but that will take some time. Add the need to belong with the need to control, and you see how tough this task can be. Many of us have been leaders in our current settings. We may be executives, we may be church leaders, we may be those who effectively run civic organizations. Joining in with those who are already at work will involve taking on a new title: servant.

We need to be reconciled to those already living out ways of justice, of which some of us are only now becoming aware. When Jesus wanted to demonstrate what it meant to follow him, Scripture says he rose from the table, grabbed a towel, and washed his disciples' feet. Maybe this act of servanthood is the best model we can recommend. With humble hearts, we need to ask those who are already skilled in the work of justice how we might serve them and become a part of what is happening.

Another key thing we need to do is pray for forgiveness with a true heart of repentance. For too long, many of us have been complacent in our lives, just like the people of God were in the Old Testament. We forgot to do the work we were supposed to be about. We did a lot of things in God's name: perhaps we led the church building fund, sang on the worship team, figured out why the roof was leaking, taught people how to verbally share their faith, or prayed with the intercessors each Sunday before the service. But as the parable of the sheep and the goats points out, God's baseline for service may be different than ours.

For some time now, throughout America many have been engaged in caring for those in need. It is our task, as the new kids on the block, to acknowledge their contributions, repent for our lack of engagement, and ask how we might help.

MEDITATION BY MARIA KENNEY

The wisdom of our brother and forefather, St. Augustine: "In essentials, unity; in nonessentials, liberty; in all things, love." Because of unity, we gather the strength and encouragement for the task we have been given; through it, difference is reborn as beautiful abundance. Because of liberty, we can offer our truest selves and become vulnerable to those with whom we have chosen to toil; through it, all of the gifts of God's children may find expression. And because of love, we are girded and bound by the Alpha and the Omega, by the before-us and after-us God; through it, our hearts are broken but not destroyed, our selves given to new life that is both dangerous and beloved.

These three remain, and in them we find ourselves, and the other, and God. Thanks be to God. Amen.

9 | LOCATION AND THE THEOLOGY OF PLACE

Matt kept a careful eye on Christine the next week as she began purging her belongings, searching for, he thought, a way to expunge pieces of the grief she felt over losing Antoine and how it seemed to bring Amy's death on afresh.

"I should have done more." She said those words over and over again. To herself, to him, to Jenna, who had proven herself the rock she promised to be. "I didn't know it would hit me like this. It seems silly almost. Just a little boy I've seen for an hour every other week." And she would break down in tears, again crying that she hadn't done enough.

"But when is enough enough?" Matt asked Randy the next Sunday after church. "Christine did more than most people would do. You know she took care of his school supplies and school uniform. And every other week, he'd follow her around that mission, talking her head off. Antoine really was a funny little kid."

Matt could see the round wheat-berry eyes, so expressive in a face that smiled lavishly when compared to its meager surroundings. He felt himself begin to break down, right there in the church parking lot, right in front of Randy, God, and the people who thought they'd gone crazy.

So this was justice? Grief and helplessness and heartache? Burying little boys who held the promise of hope in their grip? Was this really what it was all about?

◻

Months later, in culling most of her belongings—in the storage areas of the basement, the garage, the attic, even the garden shed—Christine realized something about herself she never had before. She spent loads of money. And when she did that, she kept herself from helping others the way Jesus wanted her to. Love your neighbor as yourself—not less than, or with your leftovers, but as. What would that look like, actually? *And who is my neighbor, Lord?*

Well, it didn't take a theological heavyweight to figure out just who the neighbors were Christ was talking about. Of course, the "love your neighbor" thoughts had been going along for the ride for over a year. And the question "But how?" kept surfacing.

Jenna listened patiently on Sunday after church as Christine asked her this very question. Randy suggested a spur-of-the-moment lunch in the park, so they picked up a rotisserie chicken, a container of salad from the store's salad bar, and some juice. The kids were already hopping like fleas around the playground, returning for a bite every few minutes. Matt and Randy stood over by the swings with the younger kids.

Christine topped off their cups with the juice. "My neighbors seem to need my love about as much as I do theirs, Jenna, at least judging by how much we actually see each other."

"I know what you mean. In a new neighborhood like ours, there's exactly one older couple, and they're pretty well-preserved."

"So I have to wonder if we're living in the right place. Yeah, yeah"—she knew what Jenna would say—"I know not everyone can move downtown, and surely our neighbors' souls are worth something. There's spiritual poverty and moral poverty, and

143

so many kids spend a small amount of time with their parents and have no guidance—"

"Man! You have been thinking about this a lot!"

"I know, Jenna. I'm really torn. My heart is with kids like Antoine. I can't tell you how much I miss that kid. I just don't know."

Toby practically slid into the picnic table, grabbed a slice of cucumber, and sped off. Laurel found a friend from school, and they were swinging—well, not really swinging, but sitting there with their shoes brushing the ground, chatting about girl things—like boys.

Jenna reached for a cucumber too. "What does Matt say?"

"He's been great. Finally. Something sort of snapped in him at Antoine's funeral. He loves the way we've been paring down, and now we can see we've got way too much house. He said he'd be glad to look downtown. I mean, he commutes down there anyway. That alone would give him ninety minutes of his day back."

"The best thing you can do is look around, gather the facts, the possibilities, and see what God says to you. But if you don't at least see what the possibilities are, I think you'll continue on in frustration."

"I'm with you there."

◻

Christine hopped on realtor.com like she'd done a thousand times before and began looking at houses downtown in the vicinity of the mission. Already she had made three appointments for the following weekend to walk through some houses. She knew other kids like Antoine who just needed a friend, someone to laugh with and follow around.

After the trip downtown to three houses Christine couldn't imagine living in (and really, people actually live like that?), a message waited on her voice mail from her neighbor three doors down, whom she often carpooled with to Laurel's ballet class.

"Christine, it's Molly. I just wanted to tell you that the diagnosis came back. It's cancer. I don't know what I'm going to do."

She called Molly back right away, and several minutes later, she sat in Molly's formal living room, crying with her as she held her in her arms.

◻

Christine called Yvette at nine that night, telling her about Molly and about their thoughts of relocating. "We were thinking about moving closer to the mission."

"But?"

"Molly starts chemo next week, and who knows what's down the road for her and her family? Her husband, Neil, is kind of a jerk, if you want to know the truth. When she told him, he asked if that meant she was going to have to stop working."

Christine sat on the tree swing at the corner of the yard. Autumn had finally settled in, and the leaves of the oak under which she sat fell around her. A full moon hung low and golden in the sky, mellow yet somehow concerned. Like God was watching.

"Baby, I think you need to think twice about moving down here. You know, the Lord doesn't need everybody to pick up and move from where they are. In fact, that would be a downright disaster."

"But we're so needed down there!"

"You're not going to save this neighborhood, one. Two, people need to hear the word out where you are. Know that God cares about folks in the mission. You need to show them the way, but you can't do that from here, honey. If you're only next door, you'll get sucked into serving here just like you should, and suddenly the vast possibilities for resources will be cut off. We need you to spread the word."

"I guess I just keep up with the present game plan then."

"I'd say you're doing just fine. Think of how many people you love now that you didn't before."

"Is that maybe a barometer?"
"Oh, Chrissie. It sure is."

❏

The next morning Christine baked muffins for Molly's family and showed up on their doorstep at seven a.m. Even Neil, rude Neil, was thankful.

But she still didn't like the guy.

GO AND MAKE DISCIPLES

Everyone knows the three most important words in real estate: location, location, location. The same is true for works of justice. Where you will be involved in the work of God is absolutely critical to consider.

One of the biggest temptations when people begin to think about living justly is to believe they need to leave where they are and move to where they perceive works of justice to be happening. We think this is an incomplete view, particularly for those living out the Christian story. An important Bible passage for us to remember is the Great Commission, which conveys the call of Christ: "Go therefore and make disciples of all nations" (Matt. 28:19).

Let's look at the word "go" first. The word is given in a passive voice and could best be translated "as you are going." Jesus realized that his disciples would be leaving Jerusalem. He also realized that, to paraphrase the great Yogi Berra, "wherever they went, that's where they would be." So he inspired them toward missional movement, but he also let them know that in whatever location they found themselves, their involvement in the work of the kingdom was crucial.

We feel some contemporary thinking about missions has created a dynamic that works against this individual and communal call to work in God's field. For a very long time now, the church in America has hired missionaries, who become professional "goers." This hiring can accomplish two things. First, it creates a false sense of mission. We cannot hire someone else to do missions, at least not to the exclusion of those doing the hiring. All who claim to follow Jesus are to be involved in making disciples. No one is exempt no matter how much money they throw into the offering plate on missions Sunday.

Second, hiring missionaries tends to create a false sense of location. In this dynamic, we come to see the work of God as happening in foreign lands or in depressed urban or rural areas of America. This does not seem to be in keeping with the life of Jesus. One of the amazing aspects about the life of Christ is that wherever he went, he found something to redeem. Of all the miracles Jesus performed, only one—the cursing of the fig tree—was not an act of restoration. As he was going, he was restoring.

Therefore, if we are following the model of Christ, "going" means participating in God's work of restoration. This implies a very personal involvement for what it means to make and to be disciples of Jesus.

Throughout the Gospels, Jesus called his followers to imitate him. And how did Jesus act? He washed feet, he served food, and he cared for those in need. Yes, he preached, but it was almost always done in tandem with serving others. To use a phrase by St. Francis of Assisi, "Preach the gospel wherever you go, and use words if necessary."

Serving others, restoring health to those in need, giving food to the hungry and dignity to the oppressed and the despised—these were the marks of the ministry of Christ. He regularly called his disciples to be like him, and one of his final instructions was for his pupils to teach even more people to live in this way. That was the heart of what Jesus was trying to create—a people who lived in a particular way and taught others to live similarly. At the heart of this way of living was service in the work of restoration. Do followers of Jesus tear down or build up? Hurt or heal? Hoard or give?

As we have already said several times, living in service to others preserves the way God has always called people to live. There are, after all, more than three thousand verses in the Bible dealing with poverty, many of them in the Old Testament. We think Jesus, rather than departing from tradition, amplified those things God cared about most. Jesus set in motion a plan that eventually calls all people to live justly in whatever location they find themselves.

Should I Stay or Should I Go Now?

To apply this practically, right about now you might be thinking, *How am I going to live justly in the suburbs? Shouldn't I move somewhere else so I can be available in that place where justice is happening?* But this is not how it works.

Consider the story of Pentecost told in Acts 2. After Jesus left the earth, all of his students lived together in Jerusalem, waiting for something to happen as he had promised: "You will receive power when the Holy Spirit has come upon you; and you will be my witnesses" (Acts 1:8). Something big did happen, when the third person of the Trinity busted the doors wide open and the power of God was unleashed in ways they could never have comprehended as they waited.

We're sure they weren't any more thrilled about waiting than we are when God calls us to do the same. It goes against our natural impulses. We don't like to wait. We like instant boiling water from the tap, high-speed Internet, microwave popcorn, and prepurchased movie tickets.

The first impulse when reading a book like this is not to wait but to dive headlong into doing enormous, "justicey" kinds of things. Most suburban Christians are almost genetically entrepreneurial, and we all tend to think if something is worth doing, it is worth doing off the charts and

149

immediately. Though not necessarily a bad impulse, it does not account for the processes that must take place in each of our lives. Throughout Scripture and church history, we read stories of people waiting. This is a vital step in our formation as disciples.

When a person awakens to issues of justice, it requires an entire rethinking of his or her life. We have talked already about the impact on relationships. Just as important is the impact on our theology.

Mission is inherently a theological issue. We believe the three most important questions to ask about mission are "Who is God?" "What is God doing in this context?" and "How can I be a part of this work of God?"

One of the problems with the word *theology* is we can tend to categorize it as ethereal or academic, and surely we should leave that to the "professionals." One of the outworkings of such thought is that we tend to separate theology—how we think about God—from mission. And if we can separate the two, what we do may end up looking nothing like Christ, who began his ministry with the proclamation, "I come to bring good news to the poor" (see Luke 4:18).

All of us have a theology. All the time and whether we realize it or not, we are making decisions about where our actions fit into what God is doing. This is true even for an atheist, someone who believes there is no God and lives accordingly. The structures we create, the organizations we join, the families we raise—all of these things flow from who we perceive God to be and what we believe God would have us care about.

The Theology of Place

We believe one of the most important understandings of God is what is called the *theology of place*. The theology of place states that God has placed us where we are for a reason. We believe there are no wasted resources in God's economy. Consider the parable of the talents and how it speaks about God's tending of resources and his desire for us to do the same.

This is at the heart of missions work. By now we hope that you have come to see living justly as a deeply ingrained part of following Jesus. The two are deeply linked by your view of God and your corresponding actions. Here is what we believe to be a deeply theological statement: bloom where you are planted. Maybe your mother uttered that phrase so you would stick it out in little league baseball when the other kids on the team played better. Maybe your father gave you that advice as a way to help you get through geometry or to keep you from leaving the college you chose to attend. Maybe now you tell yourself that in your church, in your job, or even at the PTA meetings at your children's school. But we tend to see this as a pure expression of being a disciple of Jesus. Wherever you are, that is where the kingdom of God is at work. There is no neutral place. That is good news.

So doing missions means doing the work of the kingdom wherever you are sent. And the best place to think about where you have been sent is to see where you are. God is a being of great economy. He works before you even realize it and before you sign on, and he's placed you where you are today for a reason. If you find yourself in the suburbs, welcome to your mission field.

Clearing the Way

However, there are barriers to following Jesus in the way we describe. The most obvious hindrances are all the market choices available to us in suburbia. Also true, however, is the way we do church. America is a tremendously giving nation. Nowhere is that more true than in the church. In

2000, American Christians gave nearly $269 billion to chari-
table causes. While this data seems impressive, it begins
to pale when compared with other data. For example, of
the previous figure, only $7.8 billion, or about 2.9 percent,
actually went outside the walls of the church. Then com-
pare that amount to the income of American Christians. In
2000, American Christians earned $5.2 trillion. Put these
two figures together, and you begin to realize that American
Christians give less than two-tenths of one percent to support causes outside the church.[12]

God's people have always been tempted to turn inward.
God called the prophet Malachi to speak against this very
practice. The nation had grown so callous to the heartbeat of God that when God accused them of robbing him,
they had no clue what he was talking about. "How are we
robbing you?" they asked (see Mal. 3:8). With so many
resources turned inward in today's church, we wonder if
God is not asking the same question.

Presenting data this way can tend to caricature what the
church is doing. Willow Creek, for example, has a thriving
ministry to help single women get their cars fixed. Many
churches support food pantries and homeless ministries.
So we are very conscious that some of the previously mentioned funds go directly to helping those in need. Still,
those figures should cause us to think about how we use
the resources we have been given.

Lisa and I participate in a project called the Relational
Tithe. This began as an effort to help followers of Jesus
rethink the way in which we gave a portion of our financial
resources to help those in need. In the Relational Tithe,
members contribute to the group. When someone becomes
aware of a concern—a need of a group member or, more
often, a need of someone we are connected to relation-
ally—it gets presented to the group. If three or more members approve of meeting that need, and if it is in the scope
of resources currently on hand, it gets met.

The key to the Relational Tithe is in the first word—relational. No needs are met for those with whom a member is not in direct relationship. Still quite small—thirty members actively participate—the project is nonetheless one effort to provide an alternative but quite efficient means to connect with those in need, providing resources in a manner that seeks to further God's work in this world.

This is one simple step that some of us have taken to engage in God's work in a very practical way. It doesn't require a big commitment. Those in the Relational Tithe already connected with congregations maintain those ties. But it provides some clear thought about how to begin living justly right where you are.

Simple Steps

We would suggest some even simpler steps. We talked earlier about the issue of mountaintop removal. One of the reasons there is such a need for so much coal is because of the immense energy usage of our country. To supply that much coal, we are blowing apart mountains throughout the country (see http://en.wikipedia.org/wiki/Mountaintop_re moval). And while doing so is spoiling the beauty of creation in those areas, the most significant concern is that if you destroy the Appalachian ecosystem, which is the second most diverse ecosystem on the planet, you will wreak havoc on the systems downstream. Already throughout Kentucky, West Virginia, and Tennessee there are places where people cannot drink the water. In this way, the consumption of energy in our homes is actually related, and not all that remotely, to whether a child has clean drinking water in the American Southeast.

So, while you might wish to be involved directly in heroic acts of service, our suggestion is to begin where you are and see every step you take as contributing to a world of justice. For example, you probably shower every day. However, we believe a day is coming when our world will fight over water the way we currently fight over oil. Perhaps a simple step toward making the world more just is to shower less. For some of you, that might seem gross. But unless you work in a factory or on the farm, chances are you don't need to get under the water every day. You just don't sweat that much.

You can also turn off the water when you shave, in between rinsing the dishes, or while brushing your teeth, or wait until the dishwasher is completely loaded before you run it. Those are good places to begin. And that is our best advice to you. Begin where you are. Think about how what you do affects those in need.

The reward to you? Lower water and electric bills. We've found that living justly is easier on the wallet.

MEDITATION BY CHRISTINE POHL

I'm feeling conflicted, Lord. I like the safety and security of my life, my home, and my routine. Bigger visions attract me and scare me at the same time.

If I let you crack open my heart to feel injustice more deeply, and if I let you open my eyes to see human needs more personally, where will it stop? If I start thinking more about justice and let it affect how I use my resources, will anything about my life remain unchanged or unchallenged?

I want to be faithful. I want a vision for missions that's as big as your heart and as wide as your kingdom. I want to love those you've befriended. But I'm not so sure about the specifics.

Could you help me open the doors of my heart and home a little wider? Could you teach me to respond to opportunities for ministry as gifts rather than as interruptions in my carefully scheduled day? I need more of your heart, Jesus, before I can give my time, resources, choices, and places to be used for your purposes.

I know I'm not alone in this. Help me with the power and wisdom of your Spirit and with the community of your people.

Dear God, I'm feeling conflicted—but I'm listening.

10 — Joining with Justice

C hristine hefted the pot of Matt's famous chili off the cooktop and carried it to the table they'd decorated at the end of the driveway. The glittery wings strapped to her back, fluttering above the tulle of the fairy costume she'd quickly put together that day, caught the porch light. She set the pot down beside bowls, cutlery, napkins, brownies, and cupcakes the kids had frosted earlier in a Day-Glo orange. Votive candles jumped in the late October breeze. In just a few minutes, as happened every year in the neighborhood, families would emerge from their homes dressed in costumes that ran the gamut from gruesome to trendy to classic.

Matt trudged over with all the lawn chairs they owned and formed a semicircle of seating for neighbors to gather. In the middle sat one of Clifton's buckets, the handle decorated with a ribbon sporting an autumn motif.

He opened up the last chair. "Almost time. This was a great idea. It's good to see if we can get the neighborhood involved."

Christine sat down in her favorite sideline chair and placed a mammoth bowl of candy in her lap. "This is the only night of the year the neighborhood comes out like this. I can't believe we've ignored it. Hopefully they'll forget last year's darkened porch."

"You said it. I hate to admit it, but it does beat trunk or treat at church." Matt rolled his eyes.

As the parade began, the first characters arrived, dressed as a tiny angel and a bunny. More children filed by as their parents stopped to have a drink, some of them enjoying a bowl of chili and introducing themselves.

Christine's mom arrived to sit and chat. She eyed the bucket and gave a little *tsk*. But that was all. Christine could handle that.

"What's that bucket for?" asked a man named Dave, who was dressed in a business suit and wearing plastic fangs. Well, he'd been wearing the fangs when he walked up. But he hadn't had a chance to eat supper. He was glad for the food, and when Christine's next-door neighbor, Barbara, offered to take his kids with her, he happily agreed, removing his fangs and lowering his tired frame into a chair.

Matt told him about the mission, about Clifton.

"I love that guy! Sure, I'd be glad to help." He reached into his front pocket and threw in some bills.

Christine was amazed at how much was given at the end of the night, and how many people, who'd been neighbors for years, she'd met for the first time.

Her mom kissed her as she got into her car. "See, Chrissie? You can still help down there and do it up here."

At 8:30, after the costume parade calmed down and all the participants had retreated back behind the mellow glow of their windows, Matt picked up the blue rubber tub of dirty dishes. "That went better on more levels than I even knew to hope."

Christine stacked up the rest of the items on the table in Zach's stroller. "I feel really convicted, though. Do you realize how many neighbors we don't know?"

"Yeah, pretty bad."

"I mean, they are our neighbors." Christ's words rang in her ears again. "Did you realize there were three divorces on one cul-de-sac alone last year? Where were we? I didn't even find out about it until tonight."

"I know, babe." They walked up the drive together.

Christine rolled the stroller into the kitchen. "We need to do stuff like this more often. This is our home turf."

"What about our other work?"

"Who said it needs to be either/or? Shouldn't it be both? Loving our neighbors right here and helping our neighbors downtown, or over on the other side of town, or in Kenya? Shouldn't it be all that?"

Matt ran a hand through his hair. Christine loved it when he did that. He had such beautiful, rich brown hair. "You're right."

"Sometimes I think maybe moving downtown would have been the easy way out for us."

"It's just different for everyone, babe. After tonight, though, I have no doubt this is where we're supposed to be."

A knock sounded at the front door. Molly stood there with her daughter Gigi. "I'm sorry we're late. I just got back from the doctor's office, and it was the first we could leave."

Christine opened the door wide and ushered them in.

"I'm so tired, Christine. And we missed trick or treat. I didn't know how to tell Gigi."

Luckily Gigi was only four, and she loved chocolate. Christine always gave out chocolate.

She walked to the dining room table where she'd deposited the candy bowl. As usual, she'd overestimated how much she would need. "Gigi, hold up your pumpkin for Miss Christine."

Gigi, a solemn little Tigger, held up a purple plastic pumpkin. Purple! Christine smiled and dumped the contents of the bowl into her container. "There! You've got all the candy you can possibly hold. The kids are back in the family room watching a video. Wanna go back?"

Gigi nodded and ran like a tiger past the steps.

"Cup of tea, Molly?"

"Oh, yes. Did I mention how tired I am?"

"You did. But you can say it as many times as you need to."

The kitchen was a mess, Matt had some office work to finish up, and the kids needed baths. But Christine realized that this was a time to show mercy, God wanted her to, and those dishes would still be there in the morning. Heavens, would they! She remembered Clifton laughingly saying, "People needing help always seem to show up at the perfect time . . . the perfectly wrong time!"

"Have a seat right there in that chair." She pointed to the most comfortable chair in the living room. "Close your eyes and I'll be back with that tea."

She filled the kettle and set it on the stove. Exhaustion laid itself on her shoulders like a winter coat.

◻

The next morning was a nightmare. The kids smelled stale, having had no baths, so Matt wiped them with baby wipes and pronounced them clean. Providing cereal bars and glasses of milk, Christine pronounced them fed, and they barely made it on the bus in time. Thank heavens Zach was in kindergarten now.

Matt drove way too fast down to the office. He felt a little disillusioned, honestly. Growing up, he'd watched his father slave for their church with a low salary, little benefits, and no real hope of retirement as such. Matt had pictured himself living at the beach someday in a nice condo with a view of the breakers. Coffee and the paper in the morning and not much else to do.

But if he wanted to follow Christ, the work would really never stop, would it? Gone were the dreams of an easy life of sitting back, putting his heels up, and doing nothing but what he wanted to do, and if nothing was what he wanted, fine.

They weren't as busy as they had been when active in church, but it was close. He hoped the rewards in heaven were worth it. Sometimes, it didn't seem worth it down here. It really didn't.

He called his dad on his cell phone. He hadn't spoken to him in weeks. "Hey, Dad."

"Matty! How's it going?"

"Good." He wasn't about to tell him about the Halloween celebration. Yes, he'd grown up in that kind of church. "Just calling to check in. I've been busy. Sorry for not calling sooner."

"Son, it's good to hear from you."

He had never appreciated his father. Not really. Kind of looked down on him for serving a bunch of unthankful people who'd sucked him dry. There were a lot of folks like that down at the mission, he had to admit.

Now maybe he understood a little better.

"Can you and Mom come up for Thanksgiving this year?"

"That would be great."

"You didn't have plans?"

"Not at all. We haven't had Thanksgiving plans with one of you kids for five years now."

"Why didn't you say something?"

"You've all got your lives. Mom and I are happy you're doing well."

Five years.

That big rest someday? Wasn't gonna happen.

JUMPING IN

In this chapter, we hope to give you some ideas of where to get started. Some of these suggestions are simply different ways to act. Some are organizations where you can contribute to what is already happening. This is by no means an exhaustive list. In addition to these suggestions, we've listed resources at the back of this book, including books to continue your research.

One qualification before diving in: all of the organizations we mention deal with issues on a national scale. We have found some great local groups people could engage with, but, for obvious reasons, they are not included here.

Start in Your Home

In the lyrics to a great old hymn, the writer prays that there would be peace on earth and to "let it begin with me." The first step toward living justly is to consider small, repeatable steps that will move you forward. Below are some suggested actions to get you started. These may seem too small, almost insignificant in their impact. But taken together, these would significantly advance you along the path of justice.

On a personal, household level, one of the important ways to look at just living is through our use of natural resources. Frankly, as a nation we consume too much. Consider these statistics:

From 1900 until 1989, U.S. population tripled while the use of raw materials multiplied 17 times. With less than 5 percent of world population, the U.S. uses one-third of the world's paper, a quarter of the world's oil, 23 percent of the coal, 27 percent of the aluminum, and 19 percent of the copper. Our per capita use of energy, metals, minerals, forest products, fish, grains, meat, and even fresh water dwarfs that of people living in the developing world.[13]

Americans are those folks at the party who talk too loud and eat all the snacks. As a nation, we are gluttons for natural resources. So here are a few places to begin changing these patterns.

Drive responsibly. One University of California study estimated that Americans spend an average of 80 minutes a day in their cars,[14] a figure nearly double twenty years ago. Add to this the enormous spike in gas usage in up-and-coming nations like China and India, and you begin to see the magnitude of this usage.

Heavy oil usage would be fine if it were renewable. It is not. Oil, like all other resources, is subject to a peak, the point in time when more than half of a resource has been consumed and it becomes increasingly and prohibitively more expensive to gather the remaining material. Some experts believe we crossed that line sometime in the 1960s, while others believe that point is more than twenty years away. Regardless, it is not a matter of *if* oil will be too expensive to use affordably, but *when*. It should come as no surprise, then, that as worldwide consumption of oil has increased, so have conflicts over this natural resource. So in a very real way, what you drive and how much you drive is directly related to whether there is conflict in the world.

What should you do about this? The easiest step is to conserve trips. Put a notepad in the car and start tracking the amount of time you drive. See if you can shave off a few minutes each week. Make it a competition with your spouse or your kids.

Another easy step is to get out that bike. I (Will) have started riding my bike to easy-to-reach places like our community building and the library. Not only will you be helping make the world more just, you will also be making yourself healthier.

Other suggestions: stick to your nearby grocery store and pharmacies. Are you driving more than twenty or thirty minutes to work or church several times a week? Consider carpooling with people in your area.

A more aggressive step is to change your car to a hybrid or other form of fuel-efficient vehicle. This is, of course, a privilege of the wealthy. We cannot yet afford a hybrid and, with three kids in the house, still require two cars. However, one of our goals for the next two to three years is to switch over to more fuel-efficient vehicles.

Eat responsibly. Food is at the heart of every culture. We talked quite a bit about this in chapter 6, so now we will focus on a few easily implemented suggestions.

Among the best food advice we can give you comes from Michael Pollan, author of the eye-opening book *The Omnivore's Dilemma*. Pollan suggests,

> Don't eat anything your great-great-great grandmother wouldn't recognize as food. Imagine how baffled your ancestors would be in a modern supermarket: the epoxy-like tubes of Go-Gurt, the preternaturally fresh Twinkies, the vaguely pharmaceutical Vitamin Water. Those aren't foods, quite; they're food products.[15]

When you eat junk, you feel like junk. We firmly believe living a life of justice involves having the energy to do so.

Living right is a function of living well, and eating processed food sabotages that goal. One easy step is to begin cutting processed food out of your diet. Read the labels. A great resource on recognizing junk is the label-reading page at KidsHealth.com.[16]

In addition to having more energy for your family, your community, and works of justice, eating well serves a global purpose. Many of the conditions in food-processing factories are deplorable. For example, some of the worst offenders of working conditions are pork processors. By continuing to buy products from these corporations, you are affirming the way they treat their workers.

One great way to combine your desire for living justly with your diet is to buy local. In this way, you can be more attuned to the working conditions in which your food is grown, and developing relationships with local growers helps you appreciate where your food comes from and the people who provide it. Two great sites to find locally grown food are LocalHarvest (http://www.localharvest.org) and FoodRoutes (http://www.foodroutes.org).

Buying local also helps deal with the problem of trash. Local food arrives in wicker baskets, while grocery store food is wrapped in plastic and paper products. In 1997, "Americans consumed 737 pounds of paper, highest in the world and more than six and a half times the world average."[17] We are being paper hogs.

If you are asking "What's in it for me?" regarding eating local food, here are at least two great answers. First, a great deal of evidence shows that local food provides greater nutritional value for its consumer. Second, as the price of gas increases, so will the price of food, perhaps making locally grown food the more affordable alternative.

Cool down and heat up. We have become an air-conditioned society. We make things warm in the winter and cool in the summer. But so much of the electricity we use comes from the burning of coal. For example, 98 percent of Kentucky's electrical energy comes from coal. Nationally, 50 percent of all electricity comes from coal. As we noted earlier, there are significant impacts to burning this much coal, including the devastation to the areas from which coal is mined. Managing your home's energy consumption is connected to whether or not a mother can bathe her child in clean water in places like Kentucky and Tennessee.[18]

Use less water. Another set of simple action steps involves how much water you use. Even steps as simple as showering less and turning off the water when you're brushing your teeth would have a profound effect on the use of this natural resource in our world.

Look Around Your Neighborhood

If we believe living justly and working in the kingdom is the same thing, then the natural progression should be to work for justice, figuratively speaking, "in Jerusalem, and in all Judea and Samaria, and to the ends of the earth" (Acts 1:8 NIV). In this passage, Jerusalem was where the disciples called home, and Judea was the surrounding area. For you, the next step toward justice, after working through issues of sustainability at home, is to consider how you can work in your neighborhood.

Neighborhood kids. In the suburbs, so many children are left in daycare, after-school care, or endless lessons and programs. These children are our future. They may not be getting the guidance, the love, and the time they need. If we really want to look forward, we need to start investing our lives in the children of our neighbors.

When I (Lisa) was young, my mother was engaged in church and political activities, so one of the sustaining forces in my life was a woman who opened her home for kids to come hang out. Almost every summer day, I ate lunch at Miss Gloria's table. Miss Gloria cried with me at movies and after the death of my favorite relative; she played games on the family room floor and took me to the pool. A simple step but a profound one, and one that we as a family are reaping the benefits of to this day. With my own mother now gone, I still look to Miss Gloria as a surrogate mother.

Somewhere between five and sixteen million kids are latchkey kids, those children who spend a majority of their time home alone. This is made even more acute by the large number of single moms and dads, which in the most recent figures is as many as twenty million. Imagine the impact on our future if you chose to invest in the lives of a few of those kids in your neighborhood.

A good place to start is by offering tutoring or other forms of academic assistance. Latchkey kids account for far more than half of school-age children who struggle academically. Were you good in science? Offer to help a kid get through chemistry. Good in math? We're sure some kid in your neighborhood is struggling with geometry. Helping with schoolwork is a small step toward providing assistance to those in need. If you live in the suburbs, these kids are probably not in financial poverty. But this step may be just what you need to begin engaging in the life of someone in need right in your "Judea," and perhaps change the course of that person's life forever.

Being a friend. Even in suburbia, people are lonely. Do you know of a woman who is infertile but wants to have children? What a lonely place she finds herself. What about the man who stays at work too long just to avoid family relationships he once enjoyed that have now disintegrated? Busyness should never be misconstrued as fulfillment. Consider Sandy, a friend of ours from many years ago. On the surface, she had so much: what appeared to be a loving husband, healthy and good-looking kids, and a leadership position in the church. Nobody knew she worked herself ragged, receiving very little support from her family and friends. When her marriage ended explosively, it was obvious Sandy had been without support for a very long time. Her case is like most people's: pain and isolation ravage their lives, and we never even know it. Maybe this describes you. If so, reaching out for support as well as investing in someone else's life may be just what you need not only to be a friend but also to gain a friend.

Reprioritize your activities. Getting involved in your neighborhood will mean getting rid of other activities that may be of lower importance. Here are some elements to consider when asking where to find more time.

- *Kids' activities.* "The average high school student spends 10 to 15 hours per week on extracurricular activities, mainly sports, but also on band, orchestra, drama and other clubs."[19] If you are a parent, you probably didn't need to know that statistic—you experience it firsthand. A certain amount of activity is good. But we fear that too many activities teach our children to be busy toward no good end. If you are looking for more time to be engaged with your neighborhood, consider how much time you spend carting your kids between sports and lessons. Imagine taking even 20 percent of that time and engaging with your neighborhood. Further, imagine that your kids came alongside you in your work with others. That would be powerful.
- *Church.* We have already talked about how much of our giving stays inside the walls of the local church. The same is true with time. Church activities can be so tempting. It *feels* like you are doing something important. And sometimes you are. But at the risk of angering all those understaffed pastors, it's worth asking whether you could find some time for the work of the kingdom by being less involved in church. Do you commute a good distance to your church? Per-

haps finding a neighborhood fellowship would free up much-needed time, and you'd become more involved in your community as well.

- *Work.* How many hours a week are you working to provide all those things your family "needs," things like an X-Box, dinners out, and widescreen TVs? Is working that much really moving the world closer to justice? How would your world change if you were willing to change how much you work in order to be more engaged in the lives of others?

Engage with Your City or Area

We would recommend seeing your whole city or area as a place for connecting with justice. However, obviously we do not know everything that is happening in every city. And what we *are* aware of tends to be great work that is happening in specific cities.

What we will give you here are a few starting points for this work—places that are likely to have activities in your area.

Habitat for Humanity: http://www.habitat.org

Rescue Mission: http://www.agrm.org/missions/donate.html

Food pantries: http://www.secondharvest.org

Homeless shelters and ministries: http://www.shelters.org

Big Brothers Big Sisters: http://www.bbbs.org

Buy Differently

Whether you choose to acknowledge it or not, you are directly linked to an overall system of justice. What you buy and eat, where you buy those things, what you drive—all these decisions come together to make the world more or less just. So we thought it wise to spend a few minutes thinking about these decisions.

Consider used things. One of the most enduring problems with American consumers is the belief that we need to buy new things. There is a real high to buying something new, a distinct euphoria that comes from the purchase. That new smell. The shiny exterior of a new appliance. The crisp fabric of a new garment.

But realize that buying new products may not be the most responsible choice. We have found a plethora of ways to buy used but still nice things. Consider resale shops such as Goodwill and Salvation Army stores. In addition to contributing to a decline in the use of natural resources, you can provide financial support to organizations helping those in need.

Pare down. Or how about just buying less stuff? Look around your house and your storage area. Do you really need all those things? When we moved last year, it took two trucks to carry all the things we had collected. We began to see them as chains around our necks. In addition to having way more than we needed, all the junk made it harder for us to think about those in need.

We gave away what we could. With a little research, you should find an organization that your donations could support. For example, when we contribute things to Goodwill, we get barter credit for Kentucky Refugee Ministries. While the things we donate may not go directly toward the people we're trying to help, there may be something like a lamp available. We can barter for that to help furnish an apartment for someone in need of the ministry's help.

Consider signing up with a barter service. One we have begun using is Freecycle (http://www.freecycle.org). You can register at this site to trade or give away things you no longer need. Another great site is Craig's List (http://www

.craigslist.org). While caution is necessary when using this site, it is still a great repository for giving away possessions and making your life easier to manage.

Buy Fairly

One easy step is to begin buying fairly. Look for products with the words "Fair Trade" on them.

Fair Trade is a movement promoting trading partnerships based on dialogue, transparency and respect, and that seeks greater equity in international trade. It contributes to sustainable development by offering better trading conditions to, and securing the rights of, marginalized producers and workers, especially in developing regions of the South.[20]

Simply put, Fair Trade producers seek to do everything in their power to create sustainable lives for everyone involved in the process. Lisa and I remember going to England a few years back for an arts festival. It surprised us how so much of the church in England saw buying Fair Trade as linked with living as the people of God. This is a process we ourselves are still working through. Fairly traded products cost more, and that can represent a tough decision when raising a family. A good place to learn more is from Trans-Fair USA (http://www.transfairusa.org).

But buying fairly can involve more than purchasing products with the words "Fair Trade" stamped on them. For example, if you decide to join a buying club, choose Costco over Sam's Club. Costco has a long record of treating its workers properly. They provide a decent wage and insurance to all their workers.

For buying gift items and handicrafts, one resource we recommend is Ten Thousand Villages, which has both a website (http://www.tenthousandvillages.com) and individual stores. Ten Thousand Villages is designed specifically to sell products from developing countries.

To research the overall issue of corporate responsibility, including research on whether particular product companies act fairly in the market, check out the National Consumers League website: http://www.nclnet.org.

MEDITATION BY CHRISTINE SINE

A recent email from a young woman said she had one simple question for me. Then she dropped the bombshell: "What is truth?" Her hidden question was, "Can I question what I have been taught about God and faith?"

I began questioning God and faith when I worked with refugees in Thailand in the mid-1980s. The misery of abject poverty and the stories of atrocities turned my world upside down. My beliefs about God and Christian faith were all up for grabs. Starving children died in my arms. "Does God care?" I wondered as I struggled to understand. My early theology had no place for poverty or suffering.

All of life raises questions about truth. Questioning is fundamental to development. It enables us to look beyond our self-centeredness to the needs of others. It sends us searching for new resources that expand our understanding of God and God's purposes.

Jesus asked questions that uncovered the deep spiritual hunger within people's hearts. His question to the Samaritan woman at the well, "Will you give me a drink?" sounds like a simple plea for water from a thirsty man but opened a conversation that touched the deepest cravings of her heart. Jesus's stories encouraged questions about faith, and his tantalizing remarks challenged his followers to question the religious status quo.

To ask good questions, we must read about and listen to people who see life and Christian faith through different

171

lenses than our own. It is liberating to admit we don't have all the answers and can learn from people of different cultures and religious traditions. As we interact with people who hold different worldviews, we truly learn who God is and what it means to be Christian.

My own questioning did not stop in Thailand. I interact constantly with people from a diversity of backgrounds. Their viewpoints frame new questions that mold my life, enrich my faith, and expand my understanding of God. Aboriginal Christians in Australia asked me, "How did God view the Canaanites?" They identify with the people displaced by the Israelites. They raised questions for me about the rights of native peoples not only in Australia but all over the world.

Early Christians believed their interactions with non-Christians taught them what it meant to be Christian. Read about and listen to people from different cultures and backgrounds. Ask questions about their views on life, faith, and God. Perhaps it will enrich your faith and life too.

11 THE BLESSING

Matt had to admit that building for Habitat was a lot more comfortable for him than going down to the mission. This was the second year in a row they had helped out with the first shift of the Thanksgiving dinner. He'd slid the turkey in the oven for their own feast later with his parents, then he and Christine packed the kids in the car, and now he stood behind the table, scooping out mashed potatoes with a large stainless steel spoon in his right hand, doling out green bean casserole with his left.

The mission had never smelled better.

Yvette had been clear. "Only one scoop per person, everyone. You hear me? Somebody'll suffer at the end of the line if the people up front take more than their share."

Matt thought how that statement applied to so much in life. He'd read statistics recently of how little the church actually gave to the needy, filling up their own coffers first. And some of the church buildings going up . . . well, let's just say nobody was worried about sparing any expense. He hated feeling judgmental regarding his people, God's people, but he could no longer excuse it. Christine was worried sometimes that God would judge the church in America, but Matt told her, "He doesn't need to. We're reaping terrible consequences on our own." It was easy enough to see in their own church. Two divorces recently, three unwanted pregnancies, two kids in rehab last year.

A man in a yellow parka stood in front of him, plate thrust forward. Matt loaded on the goods, and he moved on.

An older guy named Melvin Oakes stood before him next. Soft-spoken Melvin, quite short, was one of the thankful people that inhabited the neighborhood. There wasn't anything Matt wouldn't do for him. "Here you go, Melvin. Happy Thanksgiving."

"The Lord bless you, now."

Matt leaned forward and looked up the line at his children, who were portioning out squash casserole and stuffing. They were the reason he kept this up during those seasons when he wanted nothing more than to quit, to forget about what Jesus said, to get back to a nice, normal life. Whatever that was. He'd almost forgotten.

His children were learning to be like Christ. To learn their lives were not their own. To realize everything they did mattered—it either advanced God's kingdom, left it unchanged, or, worst of all, decreased its reach. That was worth all the nights he fell into bed with sore muscles after a build with Habitat.

And there stood Britney next to Christine. The one being served now serving. He liked the full-circle nature of this stuff. It was pretty unique from the other segments of his life.

"So, you gonna gimme some of that grub, or what?"

Matt snapped to attention. Before him stood a man he hadn't seen before. A younger guy, thirty maybe, with a parched face, a long beard, rotted teeth, and an odor that almost made Matt gag.

"Sorry."

"Well, come on. You think I've got nothing better to do with my time?"

"Well, I don't know, sir."

He reached into the pocket of his jacket and pulled out an inhaler. He took a puff. "Come on, come on."

Matt plopped the food onto the man's plate. "There."

And Jesus walked away, down the line, where Christine joked away his anger and received the reward.

Matt shook his head. Man, he had a lot to learn.

174

❏

Christine pulled the Christmas turkey out of the oven with the help of her mother-in-law. Around the table sat people she hadn't even known two years ago. Clifford and Yvette, Britney and her mom, Molly and Neil, even Antoine's grandmother Stella, her grief still just under the surface. It was late. Seven o'clock, so the mission people could make it.

Christine's dad and new stepmom didn't know what to think, and they seemed uncomfortable at first, until Yvette got the whole table laughing with tales of the mission "back in the day."

Christine's father pulled her aside before they left. "I never saw this one coming, hon. I really didn't."

"What do you think, Dad?"

"Well, it's not quite like your mother and I raised you, living with the heat turned down, all that health food, and a colorful gaggle of people around the table. But I have to admit, it's a heck of a lot more interesting. You ever get yourself into trouble with all this?"

She crossed her arms and leaned against the door of the coat closet. "Yeah. Britney ignored me for a couple of months when she starting dating the wrong boy at school and I wouldn't keep quiet. That guy was bad news! We had a little boy at the mission die, and it broke my heart, Daddy. The church people don't get me much, and some of them are still mad and threatened, and they think we're liberal nut-jobs, to be honest. I get so bone-tired at times. So it's not all like today was, believe me."

"But days like today make it worth it."

"Usually they're enough."

He hugged her. "I've found in my life, honey, that God tends to send us those breezes when the air is too warm."

"Or too smelly?"

"Especially then. What does your mother think?"

"She's not here, is she?"

Her dad just shook his head and went into the kitchen to gather wife number two and head home.

175

THE HISTORIC STREAM OF JUSTICE

Lisa and I would contend that all the heroes of justice, people like St. Francis, Gandhi, Martin Luther King Jr., and Mother Teresa had a sense there was some purpose to their work. Each seemed driven by the knowledge that what they were doing mattered to the world of their time and to the world of future generations. If living justly in a life of service to others did not cause us to believe that, how many of us would participate?

But here again you might ask, "What's in it for me?" The first notion that comes to mind is that you will be connecting with the history of God's work. There is currently a lot of talk in justice circles about paying attention to the "red letters"—Jesus's words that are printed in red in some Bibles to emphasize the extra attention they deserve. We think this is a good start. How is it that the disciples of a great caregiver came to care so little for those in need? If we are to be making disciples in the model of Jesus, those disciples should want to care for those at the margins, just the way Jesus did.

But we wonder if this sufficiently captures God's heartbeat of justice. Jesus demonstrated what God looks like as a human being. God became skin and bones and acted in keeping with those things he had been saying for a long time. What Jesus reacted toward mostly was not the earlier call of God but the way it had come to be interpreted in the life of a particular people. So many times in the Gospel accounts, Jesus said, "You have heard it said . . . but I say . . ." This was his way of drawing people back to a life given to the restoration of the world.

Jesus is the most important figure in the Bible. But he is not the only actor. We cannot think of a novel that has only one character. For that matter, who would want to read such a novel? Consider Ebenezer Scrooge, the main character in Charles Dickens's novel *A Christmas Carol.* Scrooge's story becomes so much more compelling when we see how he stands in relation to Tiny Tim, Bob Cratchit, and all the other people with whom he interacts. Maybe this is the way to view the words of Jesus.

By themselves Jesus's words are significant and have the power to be life changing. Taken in the context of the whole story, they amaze us even more. We referred earlier to the Bible as the story of God's faithfulness to people throughout many generations. The sacrificial work of Christ could be seen as the dénouement of that story. Taken as the point of resolution of a grand story in which we are all actors, it gains so much more significance.

Now look at Christ against the backdrop of the church. For nearly two thousand years, the people who call themselves Christians have been trying to figure out what it means to be faithful to Jesus as he was faithful to God the Father.

By engaging in works of justice, you plunge yourself into that historic stream. You stand among generations of people who have been asking questions about how we are to live faithfully to God's desires for us in our time. You connect with the people of Israel, who struggled to understand how Yahweh God would have them live in various cultures where he was not honored. You connect with Jesus and the Great Commission, and you place yourself in the stream of Jesus followers—the long line of people connected to Jesus through works of care and restoration.

177

Shalom Applied

This connection seems to dovetail nicely with the Hebrew concept of shalom we discussed earlier. We talked about shalom as the state of peace that exists when we are all living up to our responsibilities. Among our duties are working for reconciliation and restoration of all relationships. We think it is dangerous to view peace without responsibility. Lisa and I are by nature peacemakers. But as we raised our family, we came to realize that there is a better chance of tranquility tomorrow if we deal with those things that cause conflict today.

By joining in justice, you make a statement about the kind of world you want to live in today. Have you ever been disappointed in some significant way when someone failed to live up to his or her responsibility? Take that feeling and amplify it throughout the world. We have been called by God to be agents of shalom. When we work for peace, we state by our very actions that we are willing to accept the responsibility to be engaged in God's work of reconciliation and restoration, and we believe another world is possible as a result of these actions.

And this is where justice ties in to the future. Some of us look back now and wonder how, even in recent history, God's people could have committed so much injustice. People who claimed to be living out the story of God kidnapped slaves, stole lands, and acted in ways that caused unrest. And while some of them lived with the results of their actions, most of the consequences we are reaping today. Poverty in Africa, an inequitable distribution of resources, and deadly diseases could be traced to the failure of the church to live up to the standard of shalom.

Throughout the Old Testament, various writers implored people to pray for and work for peace. Perhaps this is the best way for us to understand engagement with shalom activities. God is always at work, whether we bear witness to it or not. At the same time, each of us has some role in that work, and whether we choose to participate or not has deep consequences for the world we are creating. History should teach us we are creating the kind of world today that our grandchildren will inherit tomorrow. Whether or not the gospel is "bearing fruit and growing in the whole world" (Col. 1:6) is in some very real way related to how we act today. It is God who grows the field of the future, but we are participants who tend and cultivate that field.

So, what's in it for you? How about a world that more closely resembles the heartbeat of God? We have no romantic delusions about this. Working for justice is difficult. It requires time, effort, and, above all, intentionality. So do all long-term endeavors. Are you up to the challenge?

Real Faces

In the previous chapter, we tried to give you some sense of what living a life of justice might look like. We shared some of the groups and organizations that are arranging and actively promoting opportunities for suburban folks to engage with the work of God in tangible ways.

This is where justice gets fun and hard and crazy all at the same time. God uses others to speak to us in very real ways. As we seek to engage with those in need, we can learn from them.

We have come to know a woman we think of as "God's reminder." We'll call her Barbara. She loves our kids and goes to yard sales to buy them toys and other assorted things. Half of those things don't work and the other half have missing parts, and for people trying to pare down and not give our kids every toy imaginable, these items are the last things we need. Also, Barbara has an uncanny way of showing up at the wrong time. Sometimes it's during dinner. Sometimes it's when we are all getting ready to clean the house. Most of the time it's far from the best time. Funny how God works.

Yet we are learning so much from her. She teaches us about generosity with the gifts she brings. She teaches us patience by showing up at all the wrong times and sometimes being openly critical of us. Barbara isn't what you'd call well-versed in the social graces. She's lived an extraordinarily difficult life, and because of this, she makes us more thankful. Strangely enough, our relationship with her is one of the real benefits of being engaged in justice.

A life of justice can be one of great frustration. People in need don't always act the way you wish they would. Despite this, we count the real faces of those we work with as one of the greatest joys of being engaged in justice. This joy is another great answer to the "what's in it for me?" question.

But the greatest reward for doing this work is to join with Jesus. Jesus never wrote a book. He never painted a great work of art. He did not leave us a symphony or the plans to a beautiful building. What Jesus left us was a series of relationships. By joining with justice, we are claiming to be a part of two thousand years of interconnection with God incarnate, the people he ministered to, and the people they in turn ministered to, down through the generations. Our lineage of faith relationships literally goes back to the Lord himself.

The great part of the story of Jesus is that many of us—certainly Lisa and I—believe that he was God incarnate. God himself joined with creation. He took on flesh and blood and lent a hand to a world deeply in need of redemption and restoration. When we participate in the work of caring for the poor, the sick, and the marginalized, we speak publicly to our identification with that work.

Believing is cheap. People in America believe in all sorts of things. When we demonstrate that belief by genuine service to others in need, we show that we take that belief seriously. But more importantly, we get to reap the benefits of knowing we are workers in God's field. This is certainly what Jesus claimed.

By joining with Jesus, we get the opportunity to actually serve Jesus. This is the paradox of caring for the least of these. On the one hand, we join with Jesus. On the other hand, every meal we serve, every person we clothe, every situation in which we minister, Jesus said, "you did it to me" (Matt. 25:40).

MEDITATION BY LUCI SHAW

Being a writer, I recognize my need to be tied to human realities that exist whether my ideas take shape or not. Jesus was. I'm his struggling follower. My efforts fall short, though I come from a human family that cares for the larger human family. Parents—missionaries in the Solomon Islands. Brother—a pathologist in a mission hospital in Kabul, Afghanistan. Daughter—an oncology nurse, giving loving comfort to those near death. Son—a physician in a clinic for the homeless and hopeless.

And I? I'm a writer in the ivory tower of the mind. Last year I offered a homeless woman at our Sunday school picnic a meal, a shower, and a bed for the night. She brought fifteen plastic bags of belongings and locked the guest room door, refusing to leave in the morning. I discovered that she'd made the rounds of all the churches in town for many years, declining help from several agencies, living in a cycle of neediness and refusal.

I felt the anguish of inadequacy. Last year I spent time work-shopping with poets in Romania, desperately poor artists who believe in the power of poetry to speak to the spiritual deficit of their recovering country. Being *with* them, receiving so much more than I could give, I felt the heartbeat of Jesus joining us and experienced the deep joy of being part of his body.

I'm still trying to figure out if God is calling me to feed bodies or minds. Or both. If Jesus were homeless, would I respond?

12 THE MAGIC POTION OF JUSTICE

Christine pulled up into her mother's driveway. She inhaled from the bottom of her lungs as she pushed the gearshift of her station wagon into park.

Okay. Just a minute more, maybe two.

For two years she'd been pasting smiley-face paper over the moldy mess of her relationship with her mother. The woman, though in perfect health, had fallen onto the path of emotional manipulation, strewing guilt, fear, and "disappointment" around Christine like glass confetti.

"You care more about all those people than you do about your own mother, Christine. And you leave me to care for the kids all the time so you can go gallivanting all around town, acting like a prima donna or something."

Christine felt caught between a rock and a hard place. If she didn't take the kids over, she was accused of not trusting her mother with her children; if she did, she was infringing on her mother's time, using her for her own ends.

She'd spent many evenings in tears after talking to her mother on the phone. Finally Matt, who normally accepted their rule of "You deal with your family, I'll deal with mine," told her that if she didn't lay down some boundaries and have an honest talk with her mother, he would.

Resentment gathered for about a week after that until Christine's mom pulled something out of her bag of tricks that surprised even her daughter. Three days earlier, before a quick visit with Britney to look over some college applications, Christine had swung by her mom's to drop off the kids. She knew she'd only be gone an hour and could easily take them with her to Britney's, but her mother had insisted on taking them and meeting her at the park afterward. She seemed extra bright when Christine saw her, a little sparkle to her eye, a little mischief maybe, but more life than usual.

Upon arriving at the park, Christine saw no sign of her children or her mother. It was almost like a scene out of a creepy movie, a chill wind blowing the empty swings. She laughed it off and called her mother's cell phone. No answer.

An hour of calling and running around went by, Christine's frantic eyes darting left and right, until finally, her mother rang her cell phone. "We're at the bowling alley."

"Why didn't you answer your phone?"

"I wanted you to see how you'd feel if your children were suddenly gone, Christine. I mean, you put them in danger all the time. How did it feel?"

Christine stormed over to the bowling lanes and gathered the kids in the middle of the game, and she hadn't spoken to her mother since.

Now, gathering these thoughts to be put to good use, Christine placed her hand on the door latch and pulled. It wasn't going to get any easier.

Walking by her mother's maroon sedan in the driveway, bare winter flower beds lining the walk, she offered up a pleading prayer for wisdom and compassion and the ability to be strong yet gentle. Mercy didn't mean letting people run all over you; mercy didn't mean enabling destructive behavior; mercy didn't mean letting perfectly able people take advantage of you. If she'd learned anything over the past couple of years, she'd learned that.

She knocked on the door. A minute later the curtains at the front window moved aside. She waited some more. No answer.

Well, not today. She wasn't going to let this fester a minute longer.

She jostled her key ring in her hand, exposing her mother's house key. She plucked it up with her fingers and ground it into the lock. Opening the door, she called, "Mom?"

"Oh, hi, dear! I'm back in the kitchen. I must not have heard you knock."

So she was going to play make-believe.

No, definitely not today.

She threw her purse on the hall table and walked past the staircase, down the hall, and into her mother's sunny kitchen. Her mother sat at the trestle table, the same table where she'd helped Christine with school projects, the same table on which they had mixed up brownies for youth group bake sales, the same table Christine had sat at with Dad and Amy to play Scrabble while Mom clipped coupons or wrote letters to her relatives in New Mexico.

"We have to talk, Mom."

"Oh, don't tell me you're still mad at me for my little prank."

She sat down. "It wasn't little, Mom. It was cruel. And if we don't get this ironed out, all of this, I don't know how our relationship will survive."

"I think you're being a little overdramatic."

"And you weren't?"

"Somebody needs to get through to you, Chrissie. You've turned into a loony."

"Like it or not, Mom, this loony is all you've got left."

"I don't want to talk about this right now."

"I'm not leaving until you do."

Her mother pursed her lips as Christine began to speak, sharing her heart for people, for what God was doing in their lives. And the kids downtown—they could be so great. Christine paused to allow her to respond at times, but nothing came. "I have to be true to God's calling on my life, Mom."

Her mother laid her hands flat on the table. "Well, I don't happen to think it's your calling, but I guess I don't have a say in the matter, do I?"

"You've had plenty of say."

"And you haven't listened to a word of it."

"Why can't you support me in this?"

"I think you've gone over the edge."

Christine rose and poured herself a cup of coffee. "Can we at least call a truce? Can you at least not fight against me?"

"I'm not doing that." Her lips remained firm.

She sipped the lukewarm drink and then set it down. "Then I guess I'd better go."

"Will you be back?" Her voice trembled, and Christine looked at her mom, the frightened, lonely woman who grasped so tightly she cut off the blood flow, who'd always spoken her mind and most likely wouldn't be able to stop.

"Yes. But I'll tell you this, Mom. You can say what you want, but I have an even greater authority to obey, and I won't let it bother me anymore. I'm done trying to please God and you. I can't do both. You know there's really no choice."

She stood up, kissed her mother on the cheek, and walked out of the kitchen.

On the way home, she called Matt. "I don't think she's going to change."

"I'm sorry, babe."

"But I will, Matty. I have to. I still love her, and I'll care for her and be there for her, but I've got boundaries to keep. I guess I didn't realize it was always up to me."

THE DANGER OF THE "SILVER BULLET"

Obedience is costly. Not everyone will understand, especially when they feel that your effort is not producing results. This is part of the countercultural call to justice. The American suburbs are often driven by the quick-fix mentality. Don't like your old home? Then buy a new one. Don't like your neighbors? Then move into a gated community.

But hopefully by now you realize that there is no quick fix, no silver bullet. The concept of a silver bullet is rooted in the legend of the werewolf. It could be taken down only with something made of silver, so the hope was that one shot would solve the problem.

But the silver bullet is more than some antiquated tale; it is the ethos of our culture. Turn on the TV after hours, and you will be flooded with infomercials promising a solution to your financial problems in a matter of days, weeks, or months. States fund significant programs such as the school system based on statewide lotteries that could be seen as preying on those most in need. The lottery mentality permeates this culture all the way to the suburbs. Unwilling to wait for the right answers or to work for a future reality, we take the choice that seems to involve the least amount of pain and provide the swiftest solution.

Do you ever buy any of the self-help books so prominent at American bookstores? Implicit in so much of our literature these days is that the author has a solution to your problem. I (Will) have a "personal growth" library full of this stuff, all cloaked in familiar language. These books have titles that begin something like *Ten Ways to . . .* or *The Twelve Qualities of . . .* You get the idea. Deeply rooted in our modern culture is the belief that if something worked in one person's life, then systematizing that process and offering it to others would guarantee success in their lives. How I wish that were so.

We have sold our hopes to the promises of the quick fix. We embrace each new technological revolution with enthusiasm. In the church, we often embrace each new church growth idea with the same level of enthusiasm. Perhaps you think that living justly is the new marketing method to grow your congregation. But issues of justice run deeper, right to the very heart of a God desperately in love with this world and deeply hopeful that you will play some part in the redemption of all creation.

Causing the world to be more just will require a commitment for the long haul. Some of the greatest injustices of our world are the result of hundreds of years of actions. It would be naive to think that days, weeks, months, or even years will solve the problem.

There are no silver bullets.

The Theology of Quick Fix

One of the biggest causes of our desire for a quick fix is the way we think about God. The Gospel of John contains the fantastic story of Jesus's miraculous feeding of the five thousand. No big surprise there—Jesus was always taking the normal things of life and making them better. What is interesting to see is how some of his followers reacted. At the end of chapter 6, there was a big debate. After the miracle, Jesus launched into a long sermon about the people of God wandering in the wilderness and the ways God had supplied their needs. Later in this story, Jesus would proclaim himself "the bread of life." The moral of this story was not that God would always provide for their physical needs; rather, it was that greater needs could be met in the person of Jesus himself.

How did some of his disciples react? "Sir, give us this bread always" (v. 34). In other words, "Jesus, you're pretty cool, but is there any way you could do some more of that bread and fish magic act? Maybe make it so we don't have to actually work for the things we have?" Jesus's followers were engaged in a first-century theological lottery, hoping they would strike it big after a short time following this itinerant rabbi.

This view permeates the church today. Nowhere is this truer than in our suburban churches. The term *moral therapeutism* has been used to describe the content of the average sermon on a Sunday morning in suburban America. In this view, God wants you to feel fulfilled, succeed at your job, raise kids with healthy self-esteem, and even have a healthy sex life. God wants you to have lots of bread to eat. But is that a complete view of God's heartbeat for the world?

Committing for the Long Haul

As we mentioned before, committing for the long haul is one key element in how God would have us live. Spending a short amount of time—for example, forty days—recalibrating your thinking can be a great start to the life to which you are being called. But the things that need accomplishing will begin to be evident only if you commit to working for the next forty years, or eighty, or however much time you are granted on this earth.

Committing to a life of justice is committing to a long race, a race that will never be fully complete. You will see some changes in your lifetime, but those cannot be your vista. In order to live justly, you must begin to see yourself as part of a plan that is already thousands of years in the making, with no knowledge of when that plan will end.

One of the hardest parts about thinking this way is the lack of short-term reward. It would be nice to have even a small honor, such as everyone you helped stopping to say thank you. But this is not always the case for us, any more than it was for Jesus.

A simple example to illustrate this point is the way Lisa and I use our home. Even before moving to Kentucky, we began having people live in our home. This is a tradition we have continued. Some folks we welcome are in great need. Some just need a place to stay. Some come to join our family for a period of time, perhaps to recover from some hurt they are feeling.

Sadly, not everyone has gushed with gratitude. One addict we brought into our home robbed us. One guest left dirty dishes in the sink and never put down the toilet seat. Another person we helped out shows up regularly with more needs to be met.

That is not to say that everyone who came inside our house was ungrateful. But if we lived with a view of life that expected even the simplest reward—gratitude—it would be tough to continue using our home as a place for God to minister to those in need.

The happy endings, however, are what give us hope. One person saw his life set out in a new direction in the year he was with us. The belief in the possibility of change is what keeps us pointing toward the future.

To a transactional culture, hope seems like foolishness, the same word Paul used when describing living in the model of Jesus to the Corinthian church. He said, "The message about the cross is foolishness to those who are perishing, but to us who are being saved it is the power of God" (1 Cor. 1:18).

To hold onto this hope, however, we need a new view of the kind of future that is possible if we act out the call of God on our lives. This is what one theologian referred to as an "eschatology of hope," or a view of the future that involves the world of tomorrow living more justly because of your actions today.

And this is where we would like to end. Imagine what the world of your great-grandchildren could look like if you began to live justly today. There is an old Arab proverb that states, "Old men plant trees." This is precisely the kind of hope we would wish for you—a hope rooted in the belief that another world is possible.

MEDITATION BY ANTHONY SMITH

Which potion will I drink? Red Bull or a Pinot? What will I plant? A shrub or a tree?

The everyday apocalypse offered in this chapter unveils our partiality to Red Bull and shrub planting while also challenging us to live justly in an instant world. We seem to have less time to crawl with those who have been trampled underfoot by the "matrix," a false reality that makes thingification, utility, and unneighborliness normative. No time to plant trees or to make and enjoy a good Pinot!

The quick fix is appealing to those of us who are run ragged in this world. Oftentimes the church attempts to be sensitive to this kind of living by offering quick solutions. While it is understandable to offer triteness to such harried lives, are we not a people upon whom the end of the age has fallen?

To live justly alongside our neighbors is to be captivated by God's future and makes Jesus's presence profoundly known in the world. Do we believe and live as though God suffers long—the same God that delivered slaves from Egypt and resurrected the anointed peasant king out of the imperial death grip of the Romans?

Savoring, not gulping down, the magic potion of God's justice will grace us to discern those beliefs and habits that make it difficult to suffer long in a forgetful, instant society. Following Christ in such a world is to suffer long alongside the *Anawim*, those for whom malevolence is a daily gift. They possess a deficit of faithful friends for the journey to wholeness.

Can a Red Bull–drinking, shrub-planting people who live daily on the quick fixes of *Ten Ways to* . . . or *The Twelve Qualities of* . . . faithfully offer love, mercy, and justice to the *Anawim*? Can we, with integrity, offer the kingdom if we fail to suffer long?

Spirit-intoxicated people drunken with God's potion plant trees that make a just and love-filled future more than a possibility.

BENEDICTION

Author's note: In my (Lisa) novels, I try to write stories that are authentic to the characters and situations I've created. However, in this final portion of Christine and Matt's story, I've written my hopes for everyone who decides to live a lifetime of justice. It may not work out like this, for we live in a broken world, but wouldn't it be lovely if it did?

M att walked out into the garden. His arthritis was getting the better of him, despite his wife's herbal remedies and the good food they grew. *Well, no matter how hard we work against time, it continues to age us, tightening up our tendons and pitting our bones, and Lord have mercy, it's one of those clear summer mornings that begs to be sung to.*

Then again, no thanks. Matt still couldn't carry a tune.

"Grandpa!" Christian hollered from the porch of the home they'd bought in the country ten years ago when Matt retired.

"Come on down, buddy boy! Help Grandpa pick some tomatoes. Grammie's making her sauce today."

Christine appeared on the porch, another grandchild, Toby's daughter Remy, sitting on her hip. "Get a lot of basil, Matty. I'm making some pesto too."

Later that evening, the family sat around the farm table. All the kids gathered close; seven grandchildren shoveled pasta into their mouths. Laurel, still single and proud of it, dished up fresh-picked salad. She was the guest of honor, home from the hospital she worked at in Swaziland. Yep, they'd produced a real live doctor. Matt was pretty proud of that. She'd be home for a month. "Toby, you doing okay downtown?"

Toby handed the salad to his wife, Rachel. "Yep. The work at the mission's going well. I miss Clifton and Yvette, though. But we're still going strong. Not one missed meal in ninety years."

Zach, an architect, loaded up his plate. "What do you think of Ruby, Laurel?"

"She looks great."

Ruby, as dark as the old walnut trestle table, jumped up in her father's lap. "It's the Africa in me, Daddy."

Laurel raised her hand. "One more rescued by God."

Matt took Christine's hand. It was pale and knobby now, ropy veins snaking beneath the papery skin. Yeah, life hadn't turned out anything like he thought it would the day he said "I do" to this woman. But it was never dull.

That night as they sat before the fire pit, Matt raised his foot. "So what do you think, gang? Like these shoes?"

Christine laughed. "He got them from our friend Randy."

Matt nodded. "That's right. No sense in throwing away a perfectly decent pair, is there?"

Ruby sidled up next to him and laid her head on his shoulder, eyes glowing with firelight. "Tell us a story, Grammie and Grandpa."

"Yeah!" The other kids echoed her wishes. Zach, Toby, and Laurel settled into their seats.

He sure would. For they had stories to tell. Lots and lots of stories. The problem was, which one should he choose?

He decided to start with the weather, of course. "It was a rainy night a long time ago, and a man stood at the intersection holding a great big sugar bucket."

A Final Blessing

We bless you on your journey to living justly. The questions are complex. The answers are murky. But you are not alone. By choosing to live justly in the suburbs, or in the city, or in the country—wherever God has led you—you are choosing to join with a whole line of people who, in their time, have sought to be faithful followers of God in the way of Jesus. In that spirit, we offer this blessing to you:

> *May the God of peace, justice, and hope lead you on the pathways of mercy and compassion. May you have the heart of God, the eyes of Jesus, and the leading of the Spirit as you seek to join with the work of those who have gone before you. And may you grow in grace.*

Resources

Books

Berry, Wendell. *Sex, Economy, Freedom & Community: Eight Essays*. New York: Pantheon, 1994.

Claiborne, Shane. *The Irresistible Revolution: Living as an Ordinary Radical*. Grand Rapids: Zondervan, 2006.

Klein, Naomi. *No Logo: No Space, No Choice, No Jobs*. New York: Picador, 2002.

Pollan, Michael. *The Omnivore's Dilemma: A Natural History of Four Meals*. New York: Penguin Press, 2006.

Rohr, Richard. *Simplicity: The Freedom of Letting Go*. New York: Crossroad General Interest, 2004.

Shipler, David K. *The Working Poor: Invisible in America*. New York: Vintage, 2005.

Sider, Ronald J. *Rich Christians in an Age of Hunger: Moving from Affluence to Generosity*. Nashville: W Publishing Group, 2005.

Wallis, Jim. *God's Politics: Why the Right Gets It Wrong and the Left Doesn't Get It*. New York: HarperSanFrancisco, 2006.

Organizations

Bread for the World: http://www.bread.org

Catholic Worker Movement: http://www.catholicworker.org

Children's HopeChest: http://www.hopechest.org

Christian Community Development Association: http://www
.ccda.org

Christians for the Mountains: http://www.christiansforthe
mountains.org

Compassion International: http://www.compassion.com

Emergent Village: http://www.emergentvillage.com

Evangelicals for Social Action: http://www.esa-online.org

International Justice Mission: http://www.ijm.org

Mustard Seed Associates: http://www.msainfo.org

ONE: http://www.one.org

Oxfam America: http://www.oxfamamerica.org

Sojourners: http://www.sojo.net

World Relief: http://www.wr.org

World Vision: http://www.worldvision.org

DISCUSSION QUESTIONS

Chapter 1: Life in an Ordinary World
- Why did you pick up this book?
- What has been your experience so far with issues of justice?
- How do you define justice?
- Is justice—however you define it—possible?

Chapter 2: Hearing the Voice of Justice
- Does God care about justice? How should that show itself in our world?
- What do you believe the Bible says about living justly?
- How does the model of Jesus relate to living justly?
- How can you live in light of the whole Bible in the American suburban world?

Chapter 3: Justice in the Burbs
- Why did you choose to live where you do?
- How does your view of America shape your understanding of what it means to live justly?

- Is it possible to have a government that is concerned with justice?
- What concerns, such as being labeled a "liberal," do you have when thinking about living justly?

Chapter 4: Finding God at Starbucks

- What are you already doing in your life that relates to God's care for the poor and marginalized?
- What do you know you should be doing for those in need that you're not?
- What concerns do you have in giving your resources—time, money, expertise—to the poor?
- How would caring for those in need relate to how you believe God would have you act?

Chapter 5: Why Should I Care?

- How is lack of commitment to those in need hurting our world?
- What kind of world do you dream the next generation will inherit?
- How is your church engaged in issues of justice in your community?
- How are the actions of you and your community shaping your suburb?

Chapter 6: Can I Answer "Too Busy"?

- What specific elements in your schedule keep you from being involved in other people's lives?
- How do Christians relate to the rest of our world?
- How do the actions of the church shape our world?
- What kinds of concerns in the world might be alleviated if Christians cared for those in need?

Chapter 7: Opposition from the Inside

- Which relationships in your life would be threatened by a decision to live more justly? Why?
- How can you maintain those relationships?
- How does keeping those relationships relate to justice?

Chapter 8: "Are You New Around Here?"

- What organizations in your community are already engaged in works of justice?
- How could you or your church join with those organizations?
- What kinds of concerns would that involvement raise?

Chapter 9: Location and the Theology of Place

- Do you believe God has you right where you're supposed to be? Why?
- Do you know your neighbors? Are you involved in their lives?
- Do you view your neighborhood as a place to make disciples of Jesus? How would living more justly relate to this command?

Chapter 10: Joining with Justice

- If you viewed your neighborhood as the place to begin living justly, where would you start?
- What is one simple step you could take tomorrow that would move you forward on the journey of justice?
- How would a commitment to living justly affect your daily decisions, such as where to shop and what to buy?

Chapter 11: The Blessing

- Do you consider justice to be one of your responsibilities as a Christian?
- How would living justly cause you to fit into the long stream of church history?
- What one person in your life can you name that you would consider "the least of these"?

Chapter 12: The Magic Potion of Justice

- How are you affected by the quick-fix mentality of our culture?
- How would you be personally transformed by engaging with those in need?
- What would it be like to commit to living and acting justly in just one place for the rest of your life?

NOTES

1. N. T. Wright, *The Challenge of Jesus: Rediscovering Who Jesus Was and Is* (Downers Grove, IL: InterVarsity Press, 1999), 17.

2. Fr. Richard Rohr, "Tree of Life: No Leaves, No Fruit," Greenbelt Festival, 2005.

3. Erik Rauch, "Productivity and the Workweek," 2000, homepage, http://swiss.csail.mit.edu/~rauch/worktime.

4. See http://www.oecd.org.

5. Fr. Richard Rohr, "The Spirituality of the Two Halves of Life," Greenbelt Festival, 2005.

6. Robert Wuthnow, *The Restructuring of American Religion* (Princeton, NJ: Princeton University Press, 1988), 12.

7. Michael Pasquarello, *Speaking of God: Preaching at the "End of Religion"* (Grand Rapids: Baker, 2006), 13.

8. Jim Wallis, *God's Politics* (New York: HarperSanFrancisco, 2006), 373.

9. CBS, "Overweight Americans More Now Than Ever," CBS News, December 15, 2000, http://www.cbsnews.com/stories/2002/01/31/health/main326811.shtml.

10. Daniel Burke, "Study: U.S. Christians Guilty of 'Overgrazing,'" Beliefnet, 2006, http://www.beliefnet.com/story/198/story_19894_1.html.

11. Doug Pagitt, "A New Theology for a New World," Nashville Emergent Convention, May 2004.

12. "Key Statistics on Generous Giving," Generous Giving, http://www.generousgiving.org/page.asp?sec=4&page=311.

13. Dave Tilford, "Sustainable Consumption: Why Consumption Matters," Sierra Club, 2000, http://www.sierraclub.org/sustainable_consumption/tilford.asp.

14. Susan Handy, "Driving Less," Access, Fall 2003, www.des.ucdavis.edu/faculty/handy/driving_less.pdf.

15. Michael Pollan, "Six Rules for Eating Wisely," Time, June 11, 2006, http://www.time.com/time/magazine/article/0,9171,1200782,00.html.

16. See http://www.kidshealth.org/parent/nutrition_fit/nutrition/food_labels.html.

17. Tilford, "Sustainable Consumption."

18. For more information on the impact of coal, see http://mountainjustice summer.org/facts/MJSnewsletter10.pdf.

19. Tom Loveless, "School Success Begins at Home," USA Weekend, August 26, 2001, http://www.usaweekend.com/01_issues/010826/010826schools.html.

20. "2003 Report on Fair Trade Trends in US, Canada & the Pacific Rim," 2003, http://www.fairtradefederation.org/2003_trends_report.pdf.

Will Samson is a PhD student in sociology at the University of Kentucky, where he is working on research in the areas of sustainability and Christian community. He and his family are participants in the life of Communality, a missional Christian community in Lexington, Kentucky. In a nearly twenty-year career, Will has worked as a Republican political consultant, as a corporate CEO, and in various positions in the world of technology. He serves on the coordinating group of Emergent Village, is on the board of advisors at Relational Tithe, and is an active participant in the Social Redemption network.

Lisa Samson's first novel was published in 1994. Since then she has written twenty-two books, including *The Church Ladies* and the critically acclaimed *Quaker Summer*. Her coming-of-age novel *Songbird* won the Christy Award for excellence in Christian fiction. *Publisher's Weekly* magazine has called her "one of the best novelists in the inspirational market." Lisa and Will make their home in downtown Lexington, Kentucky, with their three children, ages seventeen, thirteen, and ten.